Organization Theory
for
Long-Range Planning

Organization Theory for
Long-Range Planning

ERIC RHENMAN

Professor of Business Administration,
The University of Lund, Sweden

A Wiley–Interscience Publication

JOHN WILEY & SONS

London · New York · Sydney · Toronto

Library of Congress catalog card number 72-5724

SBN 0 471 71795 9

Translated from the Swedish by
Nancy Adler

Original version: Företaget och dess
omvärld—Organisationsteori för långsiktsplanering: Albert Bonniers Förlag
AB, Stockholm 1969

Printed in Great Britain
by Unwin Brothers Limited
The Gresham Press, Old Woking, Surrey,
A member of the Staples Printing Group

Preface

The research programme reported in the following pages was carried out under the auspices of the Scandinavian Institutes for Administrative Research (SIAR), many of whose members were involved in the collecting of data. Discussions with colleagues at SIAR have also been of invaluable help in the theoretical interpretation of results. Curt Berg and Christer Wallroth have provided a valuable feedback on my own interaction with various company managements. Furthermore, in their reports (Wallroth, 1968b and Berg, 1969) they have related this research programme to other research traditions. Dick Ramström and Bengt Sandkull have had a considerable influence on the systems-theory orientation of my method of description; they have also helped to weed out some of the worst blots in a first rough version of the report. Gabor Bruszt has helped to refine the extremely vague ideas about company strategy with which I began. Richard Normann's and Bengt Stymne's dissertations (Normann, 1969 and Stymne, 1970) have probably been my greatest single source of inspiration. I have often been aware that I am either borrowing direct from them or arguing against them. Both kinds of influence are of course equally valuable.

A first version of this report appeared in stencil form in September, 1968, for use as a textbook for my advanced undergraduate students at Lund University. A first Swedish edition was published in November, 1969. I have since revised the Swedish version substantially. At the same time Nancy Adler translated the original version into English, revealing and removing a number of inconsistencies and obscurities in the text. Richard Normann edited the first Swedish version, producing the final book from a very incomplete manuscript. Anders Möllander and Margit Lidén helped me with the final revision of the new Swedish edition and, together with Nancy Adler, of the new English version. The staff of SIAR in Stockholm has typed all the many manuscripts in both languages.

Working together with Christer Olofsson and others during 1969 on a comparative study of the Swedish and the American building industries, brought about some shift in my views on describing the environments of organizations. From Lennart Sjöberg I have received insights into public administration in Sweden and into the pharmaceutical industry.

My colleagues outside SIAR have also assisted and encouraged me in many ways. Einar Thorsrud, more than anyone else, has encouraged all of us at SIAR to develop a 'distinctive competence'. I have read the works of Fred Emery with much benefit. During a stay at Stanford University this

v

influence was further enhanced in discussions between Emery and myself. Emery and Thorsrud have also worked together with us on one of the projects that provided material for my report. Jay Lorsch spent the summer of 1970 at SIAR and has influenced the revision of the English version in a number of ways. Chris Argyris, Walter Buckley, Tom Burns, Neil W. Chamberlain, Sune Carlsson, Bo Larsson, Paul Lawrence, Harold Leavitt, Philip Selznick, Herbert Simon, James Thompson and Gunnar Westerlund have all influenced me through their written works and in the discussions that I have been able to have with them. I have acknowledged this influence specifically wherever I have been able to identify its traces.

I have benefited from many conversations with Professor James Howell; for several months in 1968 he also provided me at Stanford University with a stimulating environment in which I could work undisturbed.

My greatest debt of gratitude, however, is to the various companies and company leaders who have provided the material for this report but who have had to remain anonymous. In research and consultative work the greatest consideration must be paid to all those concerned. For this reason I have maintained the anonymity of all the material collected in the course of various consultative assignments; my clients have also read the relevant passages. Material has been rendered anonymous throughout by changing the branch of industry of the companies concerned, or by imposing other radical disguises. This means that the material presented below should not be used for any other purpose than as an illustration of my theoretical argument. Any reader who believes that he has identified the situations described here is therefore falling into the same trap as the reader of a medical textbook who recognizes in himself most of the symptoms abou which he reads. It is amazing how similar the problems of quite dissimilar companies can be. At the same time I have been very happy to find that my clients have not only been liberal in their understanding of my ambitions as a researcher; they have also expressed their satisfaction at being able to take part in an attempt to relate our mutual efforts and experiences to a broad general context.

The total cost of the research programme presented below has been considerable. The greater part of it has been borne by the various organizations and companies which have used our consultative services. Some parts of the work of analysis and of the actual writing of the report have been financed by research grants from the Associated General Contractors and Housebuilders of Sweden (Svenska Byggnadsentreprenörföreningen) and the Swedish Council for Social Science Research (Statens råd för samhällsvetenskaplig forskning).

In the present edition I have revised the whole book except Chapter 5 with a view to making the basic ideas more readily available. In this connection it has given me great pleasure to talk with Jay Lorsch and Larry Greiner who, during their visit to SIAR, provided many opportunities for comparing our research results with those of Harvard.

I would also like to thank Inga-Britt Aggeklint and Eva Jonson who have typed the whole of the final very difficult manuscript.

Stockholm, January 1972 ERIC RHENMAN

Contents

Introduction

Finding a Frame of Reference

Over the last five years, together with a group of colleagues, I have been making a study of long-range planning and organizational change in more than twenty companies and other organizations. The role of my colleagues and myself in these projects has varied: sometimes we have simply observed for our own research purposes, sometimes we have taken an active part in helping the leaders of the organizations to solve various types of problem. Such help has varied from the holding of a few fairly limited interviews to cooperation lasting several years. Where we have been most deeply involved, we have run frequent residential conferences, taken part in discussions with the board of directors and top management, studied the company's historical development, interviewed all leading members of the organizations (in some cases including customers and other outsiders), held various enquiries, etc. Several times we have been barred from some of the organizations at least once, only to be invited back again.

Wallroth (1968b) has reported one case study in detail. He also provides some examples of how our frame of reference has had to be adjusted as investigations have proceeded.

The postulate which has emerged in the course of our various projects is this: organizations are subject to social control and organizational problems are symptoms of difficulties in satisfying the demands of the environment. This idea emerged in stages which I will try to describe below.

Our first research project, in a business company around 1963, was concerned with the choice of strategy or, as we saw it, with the choice of direction for company operations. Our task was to help to systematize the necessary decision making. We turned our attention towards the environment. At the same time we asked ourselves: what makes one company more successful than another in a particular field? This question, and the influence of Selznick (1957), inspired us to study the way a company develops historically, acquiring a character of its own.

In an attempt a year later to identify the character and special skills of a savings bank, we noticed that certain values prevailed throughout the

1

organization, from top managers down to counter clerks. Important skills and successes derived direct from these values; so did the almost total failure to solve certain problems (Rhenman and Wallis, 1967).

These findings encouraged us to try to describe in a similar way the character of other organizations and the values they embody. As time went on, and still inspired in part by Selznick, we became particularly interested in the way the values in organizations were linked to the status system, the formal organization, the system of recruitment, planning aids and other elements for the protection and maintenance of the values.

At this point we realized that the weakest link in our theory was our knowledge (or lack of knowledge) about the environment in which organizations operate. We also felt that some of our ideas—models borrowed from Barnard and from Simon and his colleagues—were perhaps inhibiting rather than helping us. At the same time, interviews with large numbers of Swedish business leaders to discover something of the norms and values governing their behaviour, and a comparative study of some small firms in southern Sweden,[1] began to focus our attention on another phenomenon. It appeared—as we had noted but not fully accepted in earlier studies—that the existence of a firmly established and consistent system of values by no means guarantees the success of an organization. On the contrary, it seemed to us that in many cases the type of institutional leadership advocated by Selznick can be the cause of serious trouble. As a first step towards achieving a broader frame of reference and not simply describing the stakeholder system, we introduced the concept of moral and immoral environments: institutional leadership of the kind described by Selznick led to success in a moral environment but it could inhibit the organization's chances of success in an immoral environment.

This picture of the environment was obviously oversimplified and required elaboration. It seemed reasonable to start by trying to describe in more detail what I will later call the 'value environment' of the various organizations. In this way we hoped to reach a more meaningful classification of the different types of environment. I found it particularly disappointing that Emery and Trist (1965), whose descriptions of environments are otherwise so attractive, only include values when describing environments of the most complex types. In our view, the values entrenched in different environments are the very element on which a classification should be based.

Another assignment, which involved the design of a frame of reference for studying research policy in Sweden, showed us that in research organizations the value environment is closely related to financial arrangements. The type of financial backing determines the yardstick by which success is measured and punishment or reward meted out. All these factors will therefore be of decisive importance to the internal structure.[2]

Thompson (1967) has also provided a rich source of ideas. He erects an imposing system, based mainly on the postulate that organizations are 'subject to rationality norms'. I find his ideas attractive. At the same time I am disturbed by his almost total disregard of the variety of both organizations and environments. In the following report this variety is the chief focus of attention.

Further Impulses from Other Researchers
To recapitulate: to begin with we looked upon long-range planning as a type of problem solving and decision making which, because of its complexity, required the use of heuristics. Our standpoint at that time had much in common with Ansoff (1965); like Ansoff we were influenced by Simon and his school. However, in the course of our first assignments, we already found it necessary to adjust our frame of reference. We began to see ourselves as clinical consultants, whose task was to bring about changes in the management group and in the organization as a whole. Now the standpoint of Leavitt (1965) or Bennis (1966), for example, seemed to us at least as suitable as our original approach.

As we undertook further case studies, many of them very 'unsuccessful' according to the usual yardsticks, we began to develop a more independent frame of reference. I have already mentioned the importance we were beginning to attach to the values entrenched in all environments and organizations. An unsuccessful attempt to promote a merger between three organizations also turned our attention to the political systems and the political processes of organizations. Here we have been influenced by Dalton (1959) and Burns (1961). Also, since we have now reached the stage where long-range plans designed with our help some years ago can be compared with actual developments, we feel the need to explain why environmental forecasts and long-range plans so often fail to be fully realized.

Selznick has also been the main source of inspiration in our attempts to understand the growth and development of organizations. For instance, from his analogy between the personality of the individual and the character of the company we eventually developed our concept of the structural conflict. There is an analogy here with the ideas of certain psychoanalysts who regard neurosis as unresolved internal conflict within the individual. From this analogy we have also drawn our methods of consultation. The consultant must try to help the client to understand the background and history of the organization and to interpret past experience in a way that furthers the resolution of any structural conflicts that may exist.

As the gap grows between our experience and what appear to be the

Table 1. Examples of some differences between fashionable currents in the literature and our experience

A. Some of the sayings common in current 'organization theory'	B. Some tentative conclusions from our case studies
1. Strategic planning, which takes into account the interdependence of subplans, is necessary (e.g. Steiner)	1. Strategic planning is seldom necessary. Most organizations survive successfully by regarding environmental changes as independent of each other
2. Strategic planning can be routinized (e.g. Ansoff)	2. The procedures of strategic planning make it more difficult to observe and deal with strategic problems
3. Technology and markets are the most important aspects of the environment (e.g. Bright)	3. Changing values and norms in the environment cause the major problems of large organizations
4. Democracy becomes a functional necessity whenever a social system competes for survival under conditions of chronic change (e.g. Bennis)	4. To change an organization requires power to handle the political system (an inextricable part of the organization)
5. Laboratory training (T-groups, sensitivity training, task-group therapy, etc.) is essential to create a dynamic organization (e.g. Shepard)	5. Every other company president would benefit from personal therapy
6. The major obstacle to innovativeness in a top management group is insensitivity to others in the group (e.g. Argyris)	6. The major obstacle to innovation in a top management group is insensitivity to the environment
7. The major task of the consultant is to change values regarding interpersonal relations (e.g. Argyris)	7. The major task of the consultant is to change values regarding organization–environment relations
8. Feedback of information regarding moral and superior–subordinate relationships will facilitate organizational change (e.g. Mann)	8. Feedback and interpretation of the organization's history and critical decisions will facilitate organizational change

trendsetting currents of thought (cf. Table 1), we feel an increasing need to summarize and state a more independent frame of reference.

A Broad Frame of Reference

When I was working on the first Swedish edition of this book, the existence of a breakdown in the balance between economic and other forces in society had not yet become the conventional textbook truth that it now is. On the other hand most American and European researchers were prepared to support such a proposition. The situation was considered most serious in the USA, which Marcuse (1964) described as a one-dimensional, totalitarian society, exposed to what the economist Chamberlain (1968) dared to call exploitation by the private company.

> By virtue of the way it has organized its technological base, contemporary industrial society tends to be totalitarian. For 'totalitarian' is not only a terroristic political coordination of society, but also a non-terroristic economic–technical coordination which operates through the manipulation of needs by vested interests. It thus precludes the emergence of an effective opposition against the whole. Not only a specific form of government or party rule makes for totalitarianism, but also a specific system of production and distribution which may well be compatible with a 'pluralism' of parties, newspapers, 'countervailing powers', etc. (Marcuse, 1964, p. 3)

> When decentralization is carried as far as it is in Western private-enterprise economies, the individual firm is placed in an advantageous position. It must fulfil the obligations demanded by its rule as a subunit in the economic system, but these are limited. Its high degree of autonomy permits it to treat society itself—the system of which it is a part—as a field of exploitation for its own ends. It is as though a department or plant of a company were free to exploit any opportunities it could find within the company, for its own advantage. (Chamberlain, 1968, p. 141) [3]

Many business leaders share this anxiety. An investigation of the reading habits of Swedish business leaders for example, showed that Galbraith's book on the new industrial state was to many the most thought-provoking book of 1967 (Borgenhammar, 1968). Many American businessmen, after a lifetime spent avoiding the taint of 'socialism' or 'left-wing' politics, are now being taught a lesson by their children (Lorber and Fladell, 1968), just as professors are having to learn from their students.

As a business economist and researcher I have felt a growing gap between what my colleagues and I have been doing and what we ought to have been doing. But it is not simply a question of daring to break with established tradition; nor is it a practical problem, stemming from the one-sided nature of our tools. It is also a question of our own identity.

Economics is concerned with the management of scarce resources, with efficiency, with profit. Business economics describes the best way of tackling these problems in business enterprises. And, since huge areas of our world are still suffering from poverty, surely we should try to improve the efficiency of business?

I suggested a few years ago in an essay on industrial democracy (Rhenman, 1968a) that conflict between narrow economic interests and various other interests could be averted if we accepted a broader definition of efficiency. I quote the argument:

> The company is a social and technical system, by means of which it is possible to satisfy certain human and social needs. Which needs will these be? The answer will depend partly on the demands of the various stakeholders and on their relative strength and partly on the production resources and the technology available. For any measure of productivity to be complete, it must include the relation between all the material and psychological needs satisfied by the company and all the material and psychological demands made by the company on its stakeholders.

$$\text{Productivity (traditional definition)} = \frac{\text{Production}}{\text{Input of production factors}}$$

$$\text{Productivity (broader definition)} = \frac{\text{Needs satisfied through the company's operations}}{\text{Stakeholders' contributions to the company}}$$

The concept of productivity: a comparison between the traditional and a broader view. (Rhenman, 1968a, p. 128)

In the debate that followed publication of my book it appeared that at least some business executives and trade union leaders were in favour of such a broader definition. But if we compare their comments with the outcome of subsequent negotiations between the Swedish Confederation of Trade Unions and the Swedish Employers' Confederation, the disparity between thought and action is disappointing. Neither our business leaders (the Employers' Confederation is nowadays almost exclusively representative of big business) nor our trade unions seem to have much interest in any objectives that cannot be measured in terms of so much per hour: nothing is said about job satisfaction, self respect, opportunities for personal development, mental health—or whatever grand words we like to choose. Yet the Swedish labour movement enjoys international renown for its realism and sense of responsibility, its 'ability to understand the problems of management'. A report on American conditions shows that in this respect Sweden now has many followers:

> What has happened is that the union has become almost indistinguishable *in its own eyes* from the corporation. We see the phenomenon today of unions and corporations *jointly* lobbying. The union is not going to be able to convince missile workers that the company they work for is a fink outfit when both the union and the corporation are out lobbying for bigger missile contracts and trying to get other defense industries into the area, or when they jointly appear before Congress and jointly ask that missiles instead of bombers should be built or bombs instead of missiles, depending on what contract they happen to hold. (Marcuse, 1964, p. 20) ⁴

I know that many employers and union leaders share my disappointment. I am simply pointing out that we often lack the power to assert values other than those that are narrowly economic. *In practice the country's supreme goal is: maximum rate of growth for the gross national product.*

All I want is to avoid the convenient pretences that so often pose as serious discussion of social conditions. Like everyone else, we business economists have our ideological slogans. We put up a verbal smokescreen that inhibits the questioning of basic assumptions. Wisely we let others do the same, hoping that they will then leave us in peace to design ever better decision models and create impressive systems of information or control.

That some people criticize big business as the villain of the social drama hardly bothers us at all, although we spend most of our lives in the service of the large business corporations and perhaps even believe that part of their success is due to our efforts. In fact a responsible trade union movement has done more than any business economists to get the success of Volvo, L. M. Ericsson and our other large companies accepted as a matter of national importance. We have not made SKF's internal rationalization or ASEA's fight for the foreign market into matters of general concern; some of us may even have shouted with others about the 'concentration of power' in the Enskilda Banken Group, although as experts we could have adapted an old formula and claimed that 'what is good for Enskilda Banken is good for Sweden'. In fact, we should be the ones to explain that the Enskilda Banken Group is our only conglomerate of international standing; that for years it has practised a type of internal administration now being adopted by Litton, ITT and others in the world's greatest economy.

I want to break with this rule of caution. Basing my opinion on the findings of this report, I should like to claim that the critics of Gränges-bergsbolaget's operations in Liberia, of L. M. Ericsson's personnel policy in Spain, of Atlas Copco's business deals in South Africa or ASEA's in Rhodesia, are shooting wide of the mark when they criticize the leaders of these companies. These men are behaving exactly as our economic system requires. The demands of economic growth and the balance of trade compel our companies to exploit all available opportunities. In fact companies that show a greater sense of responsibility than their environment requires are often faced with economic setbacks or even ruin. Society gets the companies and business leaders it deserves.

The main thesis underlying my argument in the following report is a reformulation of this postulate: *society can get the companies and the business leaders that it needs.* In fact I have found that the companies and the leaders that society needs exist already, in considerable numbers. Unfortunately they are not used. We have worked closely together with more than twenty different organizations, and with their leaders. We have tried to observe and analyse the way they think and act. I have become convinced that these malleable creations that we call large organizations could be used more and developed further if we could just remember that they are *instruments.* That we have not let the new technology create more rewarding tasks and work places worthy of human beings, that so many resources have been wasted on producing a meaningless variety of gadgets when we could have been solving important problems, that many companies let themselves serve dubious interests in other parts of the world, that oil companies let their huge resources disfigure our towns and countryside—all this can be blamed to a great extent on a society that rewards the wrong companies and the wrong sort of behaviour. This is at any rate one of the conclusions to be drawn from the studies of long-range planning in companies and other organizations that form the basis of this report.

If Sweden could show the same enthusiasm and inventiveness here as she has devoted to the problems of the business cycle and the labour market, where business companies have become committed to the realization of social objectives, much could be achieved. Volvo and Kockums could be among the pioneers in gearing their productive processes to self-governing groups of workers; detergent manufacturers could transfer their resources from marketing to research and take practical action to prevent the pollution of our lakes; we would soon discover that many organizations, including business companies, could be at least as useful as the official government agency handling our policy for the developing countries; Esso and its competitors could be persuaded to outshine each other in building gas stations to blend with the environment instead of dominating it. And in helping to solve these problems, companies and business leaders would find great satisfaction.

In the following report, however, I shall only indirectly assume this use of organization theory to steer companies towards the satisfaction of society's demands. In the main I shall be looking at the problems from a more restricted angle, and from inside the company.

Chapter 1

Organizational Problems—Four Basic Postulates

Environmental Change and Organizations with Problems

> This is a study of a patient, who was acutely ill and who became extremely healthy. The 'patient' was not a Man but a Management, the management of a large, complex industrial organization. (Guest, 1962, p. 1)

The first chapter of a well-known study of an automobile plant opens with these words. The author tells of a factory which was so 'ill' that its parent company seriously thought of closing it down. However, under a new works manager, the plant became so 'healthy' that it was soon one of the best units in the outfit. It is an exciting story, and the medical analogy makes it all the more dramatic.

In this book I share Guest's interest and I pose the question: How can we make our organizations better? I will also make use of medical terms, speaking for instance of 'diagnosis'. But, as my colleagues and I worked together with companies and other organizations, we found it increasingly difficult to make direct comparisons between the 'diseases' of people and those of organizations.

If we say that a biological individual is ill, we mean that some of his vital processes have been upset or 'brought out of equilibrium' (Ashby, 1964/1956). But organizations are under no threat of death in the biological sense. There is no organizational equivalent of the vital processes of the biological individual, nor do organizations develop according to a fixed life cycle. These and other differences between biological and organized systems are summarized in Table 1:1.

If we were to look for some factor which could be said to correspond to biological illness, it would be natural to choose what companies usually call 'organizational problems'. To understand these properly we should perhaps look first at the problem-free situation.

According to most writings on companies and organizations in general, if I have interpreted them correctly, the Auto Company, whose environment is supposed to be competely stable, should have virtually no problems

Table 1:1. Summary of the main differences between living and organized systems (see also Appendix 1)

Living systems (organisms)	Organized systems (organizations)
They are born, they inherit their main structural traits	They are organized, they acquire their structure in stages
They die, their lifetime is limited	They can be reorganized, in theory they have unlimited life, they can be resurrected
They have a predetermined life cycle	They have no definite life cycle
They are concrete—the system can be described in physical and chemical terms	They are abstract—the system can be described in psychological and sociological terms
They are complete—parasitism and symbiosis are exceptional	They are incomplete—they depend on cooperation with other organizations—their component parts are always exchangeable and usually dispensable
Illness is defined as a disturbance in the vital process	Problems are defined as a deviance from the social norms

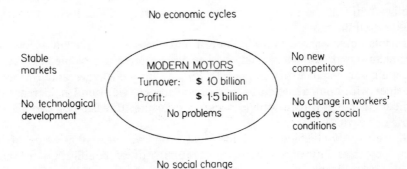

Figure 1:1.   The stable environment: the company without problems

at all. Our findings pointed unequivocally in the same direction. In one study, for example, we tried to test March and Simon's hypothesis on innovation in organizations (March and Simon, 1958). The only definite relation suggested by our material was that changes in a company were a result of critical events taking place in the environment a year or so earlier (Rhenman *et al.*, 1967). *Organizational problems are a result of change processes, and in particular of changes in the environment.* (Our first postulate.) The following are some examples from the case studies, which I will be describing in greater detail later.

Organization A suffers from reduced markets (= sales) leading to a considerable loss in profit-earning capacity, to liquidity problems and to the threat of a merger with its main competitor.

Organization B is suffering from internal conflicts: two of its departments find it hard to work together. There has been a considerable drop in product quality. B is a state-owned monopoly, but its customers complain loudly both direct to B and in the national press.

Organization C is wholly dependent on voluntary workers. In recent years recruitment has been getting more and more difficult.

Organization D is a subsidiary company, established to deal with a particular problem. Now that this has been solved, the parent company is preparing to sell D. The management of D, which had previously been operating quite independently, is reacting sharply against this decision.

Organization E has serious recruitment problems and a higher personnel turnover than other comparable companies. It is felt that this must be one of the main reasons for rising costs and an increasing work load at management level. Admittedly the increase in costs is offset more than a little by a strong position on the market, but it is felt that this situation cannot last.

Organization F has been enjoined in court of law to cease a major part of its present operations.

Company G has long enjoyed a certain amount of growth and satisfactory profits. However, a new president declares that the company must increase its rate of growth, to keep in step with competitors and an expanding market. This has made everyone aware of a number of new problems.

Organizations—Systems Subject to Social Control
It might appear that all these examples are, in the broadest sense, a consequence of some essential weakness or incompetence in the organizations themselves. However, on the many occasions when we tried to find such explanations to an organization's problems, we generally failed; instead we turned increasingly to an examination of the environment. It appears, however, that while biological systems are subject to physical and chemical laws, organizations are subject to various norms and regulations which

have been prescribed by men for the society in which they live. Only if we accept this fact, namely that *organizations are subject to social control and are judged and rewarded or condemned accordingly by society* (our second postulate), is it possible to begin to understand a number of otherwise rather awkward facts. For instance, it is often difficult to decide whether an organization has problems or not. As consultants we sometimes found that different persons within an organization have quite different ideas about what constitutes a problem. At first I thought this was because not all members of the group were in possession of the same information. Sometimes, of course, this is so. Just as often, however, the cause of the apparent discrepancy is that all business leaders are not equally willing to accept the many demands and norms imposed on them from outside the company. One man may be over-sensitive to any kind of criticism: 'There must be no stains on our reputation.' Another maintains indifference to criticism: 'No company to-day can satisfy all demands. So it's best to concentrate on growth and high profits.' In particular members of management often seemed to differ in the norms they entertained on the subject of internal conflict. To many business leaders, personality clashes and inter-departmental conflicts are always a bad thing. Others feel that while conflict may be unpleasant to those involved, there is no basic norm upholding freedom from conflict as the perfect state.

As Simon (1947), Thompson (1967) and others have pointed out, much of the social control exerted over organizations is expressed in the norms prescribing efficiency and rationality. Thompson has also formulated a number of propositions about the way in which this control is exercised in different situations. It is impressive to see how penetrating an analysis can be constructed from such a simple premise. Nevertheless, I feel strongly that further empirical investigation is necessary. What norms and values are imposed on organizations? Who exercises the control? What sanctions are available? Only after this kind of empirical examination of the environment can we begin to understand what types of organizational problem are likely to arise in the various environments and how the organizations can seek their solution.

A Note on 'Business Ethics'

There is a tradition in American research which might at first glance appear to resemble our present approach. This school regards 'business ethics' and the 'business environment' as rather interesting complications which must sometimes be taken into account. It should be emphasized that the approach advocated here is not a continuation of this line. In fact, such a line appears to be based on a distorted view of society. Its advocates have asked themselves: must business firms be subjected to certain restrictions, or is 'business' sufficiently ethical in itself? This view is governed by two ideas—in my opinion mistaken ones. One is related to the idea of 'free' enterprise. Once upon a time this could perhaps reasonably be regarded as the right of free individuals and organizations to exploit a fresh frontier country. Today 'free enterprise' is acceptable only if it means that the control of some part of a society's resources is delegated to certain organizations, to be used for the common good. The second mistaken idea concerns what Burnham (1941) called 'the organizational revolution'. This does not mean that the large organizations have freed themselves from social control. On the other hand professional business leaders have to some extent freed themselves from the owners, although this means only that social control is being exerted in another way, as this report will frequently show. In fact many of the business leaders that I met expressed a desire for more rather than less guidance from some authority outside the company.[5]

Two Types of Environmental Change

Accepting that organizational problems are no more than a punishment or the threat of a punishment imposed by the environment, and that such situations arise as a result of changes in the environment, is not necessarily going to make it any easier to prevent or solve the problems.[6]

Nevertheless, it would be an important step forward to be able to describe and classify environmental changes in such a way that problems requiring different treatment could be distinguished from each other. One of the aims of this report is to clear the way for such a description and classification. Let us look at a specific case. In May 1970 a colleague and I were discussing with the management of International Meat Packers the present situation of their company. Management declared the following to be the ten most important and acute problems.

Shortage of manpower in the German factories.

Disruption of production in the Danish factory for reasons of hygiene.

Head of the Danish operation leaving to join a competitor.

Conflict with an American Company regarding patent on packing methods.

Difficulty in evaluating future developments in EEC.

Some competitors exploiting the greater supply of qualified technicians now available in several countries.

Stricter legislation, regarding certain preservatives.

Unexpected success of new fish product causing delivery problems.

Problems with new IBM machines at head office.

Greater demands on working environment, industrial democracy, etc. in several countries.

Traditionally, in this company and elsewhere, this kind of problem stemming from environmental change has been classified and assigned to certain functional categories. Some matters are classified as personnel problems, others as production matters, others as belonging to marketing or 'general management', etc. However valuable this sort of specialization may be, it still does not give us an insight into why certain problems are difficult or even impossible to solve along traditional lines. I believe that another classification will prove more meaningful.

Organizations have within themselves special resources and methods for withstanding the destructive effects of environmental change. Overcapacity, resource buffers and control systems (within the framework of a given structure) are the chief weapons against random or cyclical variations. They can also be used to combat unpredictability and variations generated within the system. Table 1:2 summarizes the situation in a hospital that we have studied (Rhenman, 1969).

However, these mechanisms can only combat change and uncertainty up to certain limits. A violation of the limits could mean very severe threats to the organization (e.g. a seasonal drop in sales becomes so serious that the company faces a liquidity crisis). But as long as the changes are in the nature of random or cyclical variations round a stable mean, the problems involved can generally be solved in one of the ways indicated above. If on the other hand the changes are irreversible, or if they consist of variations building up to a permanent change in the mean, the limits will sooner or later be exceeded. Adaptation to such changes will call for quite different methods.[7] Permanent changes in the environment require changes in the structure of the organization. The companies that we studied were facing such environmental changes as the internationalization of competition, rising personnel costs and shortage of labour, technological development, and changes in the structure of the supplier markets. Combative measures included: a change of market, merger with a competitor, technological innovations (to counteract rising wage costs), and new forms of cooperation with suppliers.

In theory the difference between these two types of environmental change is that *cyclical changes and disturbances (reversible changes) can be met by measures based on the principle of 'negative feedback'.[8] This is not*

Table 1:2. Disturbances in a hospital, and how they are met

Disturbances	Mechanisms for dealing with disturbances
Variations generated outside the system	
Inflow of patients to outpatients department	Longer queues or spare capacity
Number of examinations required in outpatients departments, causing co-ordination problems with other units	Pressure on service departments
Number of acute cases in outpatients	Queues form or acute cases have to wait
Inflow of patients	Queues for limited number of places
Number of examinations and amount of treatment required for inpatients	Dimensioning of labour force according to peak load. Extra work or extra capacity
Inflow of patients, night time	Extra pressure on duty doctors and nurses
Time of patients' arrival in relation to X-ray department's lunch hour	Longer waiting time for patients
Absence from work leading to lack of resources	Delay in treatment
Demands on doctors' time by pharmaceutical salesmen	Patient queues
Variations generated within the system	
Consumption of supplies in the various departments	Allowance for shortages. Store personnel perhaps required to bring what is needed to the department. Use of resources or care of patients sometimes allowed to deteriorate
Differences in work load between hospital units	Under or overemployment of some resources
Variations in time spent on rounds	Allowance for possible delays in the operating theatre
Variations in starting-time for rounds	Flexibility in use of resources in the wards
Need for tests late in the day	Extra pressure on the laboratories
Pressure on X-ray department	Extra capacity or queues
Variations in reliability of filing and discharge systems	Extra pressure on doctors, possibly lower standard in case records

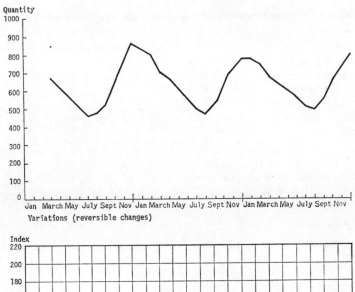

Variations (reversible changes)

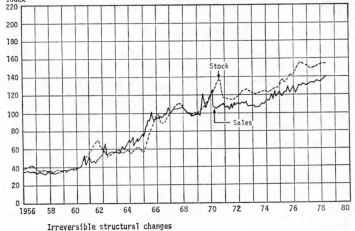

Irreversible structural changes

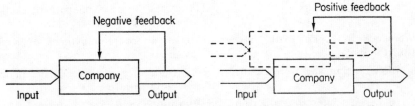

Variations and disturbances can be met by negative feedback mechanisms which restore equilibrium. Structural changes must be detected as early as possible and counteracted by some sort of structural change within the company. The term 'positive feedback' implies that a slight change in the environment often has to be reinforced before it provokes the necessary change in the company.

Figure 1:2.   Dealing with variations and structural changes *true of structural environmental changes.* (Our third postulate.) To deal with these it is necessary to recognize as early as possible that the changes are structural and to adjust the whole construction of the company accordingly. This is especially difficult because structural changes in the environment often mean the emergence of new and unknown conditions which do not match any previous experience of the organization. It is not surprising that such changes are not always immediately understood. In theory the problem has to be solved by early warning and 'positive feedback', that is by various mechanisms of learning and amplification.

The first type of problem is not only easier to deal with, at least theoretically; it has also received more attention in the literature. It is typical that we lack everyday words for describing the principle of positive feedback. While negative feedback is suitably translated as 'counteraction', we have no equivalent term such as 'pro-action'. In this report, however, we will be concerned almost exclusively with structural changes in the environment and the organizational problems that these engender. International Meat Packers can illustrate our approach.

> Some of the environmental changes mentioned by management were obviously of the kind we have called disturbances or variations. The shortage of manpower in the German factories was the short-term result of an economic upswing. The difficulties in Denmark and the trouble with the new computer were also temporary disturbances. Such problems could be treated within the framework of the existing organization; various countermeasures, such as a redistribution of resources, are possible.

> The EEC market, the increasing supply of qualified staff, new restrictions on the use of chemical preservatives and growing demands on the working environment all clearly represent structural problems, calling in some way or another for structural changes in the company.

> Particularly interesting discussions turned on the patent problem and the unexpected success of the fish product. Some members of management saw these as just two more temporary disturbances to be dealt with by conventional methods. Others took them more seriously, seeing them as early warning signals of major structural changes (the role of patents as a means of competition and consumers' attitude towards different protein raw materials).

A Note on Disintegration and Maintenance

We should not leave the problems caused by disturbances and variations without mentioning that they too can give rise to serious structural problems. They wear down the structure of the organization, acting as a corrosive. As an example we can look at the hospital where the disturbances are unusually intractable: for example, acute cases, variations in the inflow of patients, absenteeism, delayed rounds and extended operation times due to sudden complications.[9] Admittedly there are some counteracting factors, i.e. overcapacity, queues, variations in the quality of treatment, variations in work rate, etc., all of which temper the effects of the disturbances. But sooner or later variations and fortuitous changes will succeed in disrupting existing systems.

> The system of appointments often breaks down since no-one trusts it to work; nurses may fail to prepare patients in time for operations assuming that the surgeon will come late from his morning round; patients tend to arrive up to two hours early for appointments hoping to avoid long waits; doctors feel compelled to lower standards because the pressure is too great—in the end they come to ask less of themselves. Stress symptoms, low morale and high personnel turnover are all expressions of disintegration.

Continual efforts must therefore be made to maintain or uphold systems. In the hospital it was possible to identify fairly accurately the units and systems that were holding out against collapse, and those that were worn out and had been allowed to deteriorate.

> The leaders (mainly the senior physicians or surgeons and the more senior of the nursing staff) had sometimes managed to engage many of the staff on the work of maintenance, but generally their own constant surveillance played a major part. Often it seems as though positive efforts towards improvement are needed simply to keep a system ticking over at its present level of efficiency. Campaigns to improve time-keeping, discussion with all the personnel involved of possible improvements in hygiene, discussions about new and better methods of treatment, joint formulation of a better planning system—these were typical signs of an effort to maintain standards, even if they were not so described by the persons concerned.

The problem of the maintenance and 'improvement' of the subsystems in an organization has often been discussed in the literature, but without any very clear idea of the cause of the disintegration. It has generally been explained in complicated psychological and sociological terms. Moreover the problem of maintenance has often been confused with the processes of structural change that we shall be discussing later. Our own material (except data from the hospital) deals mainly with the struggle of organizations to combat structural change, but in Appendix 2 I will try to show how material collected by other researchers can be interpreted as attempts on the part of management to maintain an organizational structure which environmental noise and variation are threatening to wear down.

Ideal Types as a Language for Describing Individual Organizations

The consultant or researcher arriving in a company will often find the head of the firm very eager to convince him that this company is 'different'. This is often said a little apologetically: 'Of course we're rather a special company', or 'We've got lots of traditions we have to respect'. There has been an unfortunate tendency in organization research to neglect or even deny these differences. Only lately has it become clear to researchers too that organizations are by no means all the same and that the business leader is usually right to emphasize the special character of his company and its situation. But now textbooks appear by the dozen, telling us how organization size, the state of technology, the pace of change in the environment, the company's historical background, etc., all affect the organizational structure.[10]

In my view the methods of organization research have not yet been properly adapted to their purpose. *Attempts to establish general propositions of the type to be found in the natural sciences must be replaced by a determination to develop models (a language) making it possible to treat every organization as an individual case.* (Our fourth postulate.) Methodological precedents can be found, for example, in the work of Keynes and Freud, both of whom did exactly what I am suggesting: developed a language and models for diagnosing and treating new situations based on the intensive study of individual cases.

On the methodological side we have had two other sources of inspiration, namely systems theory and the use of ideal types as practised by certain social scientists. We can look upon systems theory as a language in terms of which we can describe not only simple biological organisms, the human body, ecological systems, small groups and organizations, but also more complex systems such as labour markets or whole nations. But perhaps the chief value of systems theory is that it helps our understanding of individual systems by relating these to other neighbouring systems. In particular we can study different system hierarchies: they may consist, for example, of individuals, work groups, departments, organizations, or markets. Each such hierarchical level can be regarded as the environment or suprasystem of the level below.

Ideal types have frequently been used in economics, sociology and other disciplines as an aid in analysis. It is hardly necessary to say that they have not been used with any normative purpose. Nor—and this does need emphasizing—are they geared to a direct classification of real-life situations. Every economist knows that the ideal cases of competition that appear in so many analytical models (free competition, oligopoly, monopoly, etc.) are rarely if ever to be found in their pure form in real life. They are simply meant to call attention to certain characteristic features of extreme cases, thus making it possible to analyse and understand the complex organizations of reality. The same is true of Weber's classical dichotomy of the rational and the traditional system of norms.

In this report too I will use ideal types as an analytical tool. I will combine them with a systems theory approach, i.e. I will examine the way in which systems at different levels (the subsystems in an organization, the organization as a whole, the organization's environment) hang together in certain idealized cases.

Summary

Organizations cannot be ill; they cannot die. But they may be subjected to sanctions from their environment. I will call such sanctions, actual or threatened, *organizational problems*. These generally spring from structural changes in the environment.

In this study I hope to show something of the way in which different kinds of organizational problem arise; at the same time I will suggest how these problems can be prevented or solved. However, my approach is geared to systems theory, which means that I do not use statistics or other techniques to support generally applicable propositions. Instead I try to develop a language for describing and understanding individual cases, for use in the prevention or solution of particular problems. My propositions are more in the nature of postulates relating the various concepts in the model to each other. My material—the cases studied by myself and my colleagues—is presented chiefly as illustrative examples. The reliability and validity of our findings can be judged according to the usefulness of the 'language' and the model presented below in the understanding and tackling of other organizational problems in other organizations.

Chapter 2

The Efficiency of Organizations in a Changing Environment

Organizations are subject to social control. 'Show more profit every year!' or 'Don't discriminate customers!' are typical social exhortations. If the organization transgresses the norms of its environment, and if a sufficiently serious sanction is threatened or has already been imposed, the organization has problems.

Thus organizational problems are an inability to fulfil the demands of the environment; in other words they are a relation between environment and organization. There has to be a prosecutor, a criminal, and the risk of punishment, before we can meaningfully speak of 'trouble'. Thus, before we begin to discuss what can be done to avoid or solve organizational problems, we must look more closely at the texture of the organization and the environment and study the interaction between the two. This and the two following chapters will be devoted to these three topics. I will in fact take the last-mentioned topic—the interaction between organization and environment—first, in order to introduce from the beginning a useful theoretical concept: the 'principle of consonance'. But before that another essential concept—that of organizational efficiency—must also be mentioned.

Efficiency

Efficiency is a useful and much used concept. Unfortunately the meaning attached to it varies. Sometimes it is used to describe a characteristic of a system, and sometimes to describe a relation between a system and its environment. I will be employing both these concepts, designating them *internal* and *external efficiency* (cf. also Rhenman and Stymne, 1965). Formally they can be defined as follows:

External efficiency is a measure of the value assigned to the products of the organization in relation to the cost of the resources consumed. External efficiency resembles the concept 'terms of trade' in economics. It is calculated as the ratio between the environment's evaluation of one unit of the organization's output and the evaluation of one unit of input. In most organizations, with their variety of products and resources, it is very difficult to make this calculation, which has to be expressed as an index.

23

Internal efficiency is a measure of the qualities of the organization as an instrument for transforming resources into products. It resembles the technological concept of 'conversion efficiency'. It is calculated as the ratio between the number of output units and the number of input units. This index, too, is of course often difficult to estimate.

Total efficiency is the product of external and internal efficiency.

Table 2:1 provides a simple illustration of these concepts of efficiency. It shows the development of two textile firms during the period 1960–1970. During the 1960's Company A automated and rationalized much of its productive process, hoping to be able to hold its own despite increasing imports of cheap textile products from Eastern Europe, Asia and elsewhere. The company managed to raise internal efficiency to nearly three times its former level. This almost but not quite counteracted the unfavourable relation developing between prices and wages (external efficiency).

Company B approached the matter quite differently. By means of successive developments in production it changed direction towards a specialized section on the periphery of the traditional textile industry. Results showed themselves primarily in improved external efficiency, reflecting the higher product prices on the new markets. Internal efficiency hardly improved at all during the same period, chiefly because of the frequent reorganizations of production. Nevertheless a look at stock exchange prices shows that Company B enjoyed the more favourable development: towards the end of the 1960's B's stock was much sought after while A's was at a discount.

Table 2:1. Efficiency development in two companies over a seven-year period

	A		B	
	1960	1967	1960	1967
Number of units produced	100	212	100	133
Number of man hours	100	110	100	104
Internal efficiency	1·00	1·93	1·00	1·28
Price per unit produced	100	84	100	301
Wage per man hour	100	201	100	210
External efficiency	1·00	0·42	1·00	1·43
Total efficiency	1·00	0·81	1·00	1·83

$$\text{Internal efficiency} = \frac{\text{Input quantity (products)}}{\text{Output quantity (production factors)}}$$

$$\text{External efficiency} = \frac{\text{Price index for products}}{\text{Price index for production factors}}$$

$$\text{Total efficiency} = \text{Internal efficiency} \times \text{external efficiency}$$

Equi-efficiency

There is usually only one way of solving a puzzle. Practical problems, such as the building of a road between two points, can be solved in several more or less equally efficient ways. In the former case we have no degree of freedom; in the latter we have considerable play. In a third case the demands on a system may be so severe that it is impossible, with the components and subsystems available, to find a solution at all. If we ask a construction engineer to design a system that will pump water to a height and at the same time provide energy, he will tell us it cannot be done.

One of the main tasks of empirical research has been to discover the amount of free play in the solution of organizational problems. According to the classical approach it was the job of the business leader, the consultant, the engineer, etc., to find the 'one best way' (Taylor, 1947). More recently it has been claimed that no such way exists. In real life people are content to seek reasonably satisfactory or 'satisficing' solutions. The question to be tackled is then one of resource allocation: how much should be invested in the search for alternatives?

I will use the term *equi-efficiency* here to describe a situation in which two systems with different internal structures can carry out a function with equal efficiency.

The Principle of Consonance

When two systems interact, the input from one system may act as a disturbance, leading to wear in the receiving system, or it may help to maintain or support the receiving system.[11] I will call two systems that maintain or support each other *consonant* systems. Two systems that disturb and therefore wear each other down, will be called *dissonant* systems.[12]

Later I will be more specific in my propositions. Now, to illustrate the importance of consonance, we can look at some situations in which various systems in an organization and/or the environment are not in consonance with each other.

> In 1966 the Construction and Building Company (ABAB) reorganized production along divisional lines. In this way the company achieved better consonance with the market, which was making greater demands on specialized knowledge of the different products. During the first year, however, the company had big internal problems, partly because of difficulty in adapting the budget and cost accounting systems sufficiently quickly to the demands of the new organization. See Figure 2:1.

> The main problem of the partly state-owned Development Company was to try to accord its own development programme with

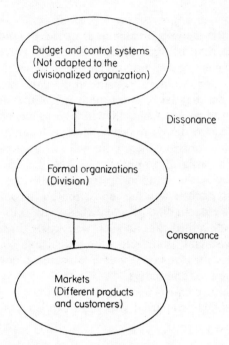

Figure 2:1. Consonance and dissonance in the Construction and Building
Company (ABAB)

the requirements of the Swedish power industry and the production potential of the manufacturing industries. The company was about to be dissolved and reorganized when it was discovered that while its heavy water reactor successfully matched domestic raw material resources (natural uranium), it did not meet the needs of the Swedish power market.

International Mechanical Industries (Inmec) had great difficulty in persuading its overseas subsidiaries to follow the parent company in penetrating the whole of the EEC market. An investigation revealed that a major cause of this difficulty was lack of consonance between expressed goals and the tools used for measuring and rewarding performance. Subsidiary heads were rewarded for yield on capital invested in their companies; with the comparatively high internal accounting prices employed, they could only skim the cream off the market if they were ever to be able to report any profit. 'Management speaks with a double tongue' one frustrated subsidiary head declared bitterly.

In the Transport Administration Office the major planning problem was to harmonize the road network with other subsystems in Sweden, e.g. the log-floating network, the car fleet, industrial location. Many log-floating routes were being closed down and this meant, among other things, that the road network needed developing. It was difficult for TAO to deal with this. Heavy traffic, trucks, etc. were multiplying more quickly than had been foreseen when large parts of the road network were planned.

The Forestry Company had many problems. Most of them arose at least in part from dissonance between subsystems or between the company and its environment. The company had been unlucky: it had built a large plant geared to the production of Kraft paper. This coincided with a period of general economic decline and with a serious overproduction of Kraft paper. An interesting example of dissonance between subsystems concerned the acquisition of some quite profitable smaller companies. Unfortunately their requirements, for instance as regards marketing, were not always consonant with those of the Forestry Company. It was difficult to adjust them to the company's organizational systems and they were soon running at a loss.

Karl Westlund's problem was partly one of location. However, on several earlier occasions the company had successfully coped with this type of difficulty. Much more serious now was a gradual change in customer structure. Previously the customers had been a few municipal or cooperative estate companies. Now, with the growing importance of one-family homes, it was becoming increasingly necessary to adjust the internal system and to sell direct to the customer. This called for a completely new market-oriented organization, in a company that had been used to devoting all its interest to the production side.

The internal problems of the hospital stemmed in the main from the following situation: because of new methods of treatment and growing specialization, a number of clinics that had functioned independently of each other in the past, now included many units that were closely dependent on one another. In the new situation there was poor consonance between, on the one hand, the planning and control systems available and, on the other, the problems of planning and coordination caused by the patient flows.

Consonance, Efficiency and Organizational Problems

Organizational problems have been defined as a state of dissatisfaction in the organization (generally at management level), caused by the application or threat of sanctions from the environment. A number of factors often interact when serious problems arise.

The Interior Decorating Company provides us with an example:

> Since the mid-1920's the Interior Decorating Company has introduced a series of major innovations and built up a dominating position on the market. Despite considerable economic fluctuations it was possible to accumulate considerable internal reserves. Although several competitors followed its example, there was no direct threat to the company. The total market increased and the company's dominating position saved the situation. But rising wage rates, particularly during the 1950's and 1960's, meant a loss in profit-earning capacity although the market accepted a considerable rise in prices. Much of the company's reserves were absorbed by various schemes for improving efficiency in an attempt to counteract the rise in costs. But management remained unaware of the problems until the board began to exert pressure demanding longer-range plans. A five-year budget suggested that in five years' time the company would be in considerable economic difficulties. Under continued pressure from the board the problems were pinned down more specifically and scapegoats identified. In particular it was agreed that the marketing side left much to be desired. At a meeting of the board in the middle of 1968, however, the president produced a long list of other acute problems: quality control, product development, financing, management training, customer structure, distribution channels, etc. In the hope that the company could regain something of its former position the board had previously suggested in general terms the acquisition of some other small companies. Now, however, another large company had offered to buy the Interior Decorating Company.

In this as in most of the other organizations that we studied, disturbances from the environment had apparently been allowed to corrode the structure of the organization until the situation became thoroughly unsatisfactory. Nevertheless, in no case was this the major cause of the organizational problems. Instead, as was suggested in previous chapters, the major cause was the irreversible (structural) change. By applying the principle of consonance we can now formulate the following postulate.

Irreversible changes in an organization's environment give rise to dis-

sonance between organization and environment and between subsystems in the organization. Ultimately this means problems for the organization.

It appears that a major factor in this chain of events is the drop in efficiency that accompanies dissonance. Thus, a lack of consonance between the organization's value system and the values upheld by the environment has a detrimental effect on external efficiency; lack of consonance between subsystems in the organization, has a similar effect on internal efficiency.

In Chapter 5, and to a lesser extent in other parts of this report, I will provide several examples of these relations between environmental change, lack of consonance, falling efficiency, environmental sanctions, and organizational problems. I have introduced the concepts here to explain why so much attention is devoted in the following pages to various processes that can create consonance between systems.

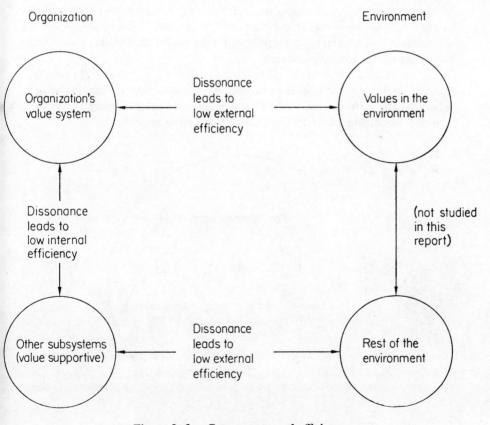

Figure 2:2. Consonance and efficiency

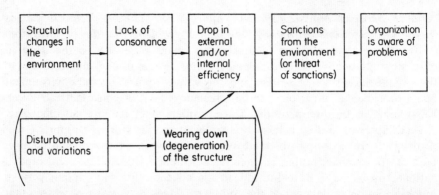

Figure 2:3. Structural changes in the environment lead to organizational
problems

Consonance—How Can It Be Achieved?

A basic weakness in the postulate concerning consonance in its present
form is that we have so far used a very broad definition of the concept of
'consonance'. A closer examination will also reveal that there are at least
four types of 'consonant' situation.

Let us call the system in which we are chiefly interested the *studied
system*. To be successful this system must in some way harmonize with a
neighbouring system. The studied system and the neighbouring system are
assumed in certain cases to have a *common environment*.

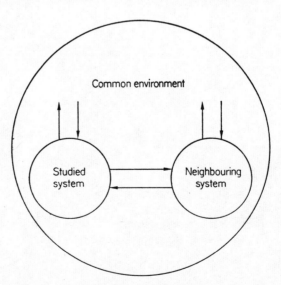

Figure 2:4. Diagram to describe mechanisms for achieving consonance

Mapping

As a first case let us assume that the studied system is oriented only towards maintaining and developing itself; at the same time it regards the neighbouring system as a part of its legitimately exploitable environment. This situation has been fairly thoroughly discussed in the literature. It has been shown that for an exploiting system to adapt successfully to a structurally changeable environment, it must be able to reflect the environment (in this case including the neighbouring system) in its own structure. Buckley (1967) has described four qualities required for successful adjustment, the ability to reflect or 'map' being the most important.

> This means that our adaptive system—whether biological, psychological or sociocultural—must manifest (1) some degree of 'plasticity' and 'sensitivity' or *tension* vis-à-vis its environment such that it carries on a constant interchange with environmental events, acting on and reacting to them; (2) some source of mechanism providing for *variety*, to act as a potential pool of adaptive variability to meet the problem of mapping new or more detailed variety and constraints in a changeable environment; (3) a set of *selective* criteria or mechanisms against which the 'variety pool' may be sifted into those variations in the organization or system that more closely map the environment and those that do not; and (4) an arrangement for *preserving and/or propagating* these 'successful' mappings.

(Buckley, *Sociology and Modern Systems Theory*, Prentice-Hall, Inc., 1967, p. 63)

> The Provincial Savings Bank had been very unsuccessful in mapping an important feature in its environment, namely the residential location of the customers, in its organization. The past twenty-five years had seen a big shift in population. Some parts of the countryside had become depopulated while in other parts of the area new rapidly expanding towns and suburban districts had grown up. The branch offices of the Bank tended to remain where the population had been several decades ago. This inability to map the environment in its own structure was a major cause of the company's problems.

Matching

In a second and quite different case, the studied system and the neighbouring system are exploiting the common environment together; the studied system will be rewarded chiefly for its ability to cooperate with and support its neighbouring system. Here the need for consonance assumes another significance, and one which has received far less attention in the literature of systems theory. Instead of mapping the neighbouring system with a view to exploitation, the studied system must instead try to understand its neighbour's weaknesses and strengths in order to complement or 'match' these in the joint effort to exploit the common environment. If the studied system can also call forth similar matching processes on the part of the neighbouring system, this is all to the good.

A good example of this type of situation was the relation of the National Rationalization Office (NRO) to the government agencies whose interests it was supposed to serve. Although in some ways NRO functioned like a firm of commercial consultants, nobody expected it to look upon the government agencies as an exploitable market. New paths to success were gradually recognized. Instead of concentrating on the development of its own resources, NRO supported a 'neighbouring' agency with which it maintained close cooperation. Furthermore it encouraged the universities and commercial consultant firms to interest themselves in the problems of the public administrators. Another matching process was the creation of strong controllers' departments in the various agencies working together with NRO.

Joint Optimization and Joint Consultation
A third case combines features of the two described above. The studied system aims at maintaining and developing itself, regarding the neighbouring system as part of the exploitable environment; at the same time it aims at supporting and cooperating with the neighbouring system with a view to a joint exploitation of the common environment. This is possible only if the organization possesses a combination of the abilities required in both the previous cases. In other words it must be able to map for exploitation and match for cooperation.

The best example from our material is Karl Westlund & Co., which to some extent exhibited this combination vis-à-vis its municipal and cooperative customers. As house-building and other construction work in the area spread from the small communities to local centres, and eventually to larger towns, the company transferred its production resources likewise. Karl Westlund & Co. was thus able to go a long way towards mapping the exploitable environment in its own structure. But, wherever the estate firms had production resources of their own, Karl Westlund & Co. could plan its resources so as to avoid duplication, at the same time developing its service organization far beyond what is normal for a building firm so as to make good any lack of equipment on the part of the other firms. The company's aim here was to combine with the estate firms to serve the ultimate consumer.

Karl Westlund & Co. provides us with another very elegant example of the ability to weigh company interests against general interests. During the building of a large housing estate, it was discovered that the roof coverings were not satisfactory. Complaints from residents drew public attention to this before there was time to do anything about it. An immediate investigation revealed that the roof covering had been provided by the builder—a cooperative firm with its own carpentry shop—and, partly because of the internal structure of the cooperative organization, it was going to be difficult to meet the demands of the tenants straight away. In this situation Karl Westlund & Co. decided at once to assume both moral and financial responsibility. Despite a consequent reduction in profits for that year, the company paid for the necessary improvements, thus solving a serious problem for its partners in the joint venture.

Dominance

When two systems interact they will immediately affect each other's behaviour and, in the long run, each other's structure. I have described some examples of this above, and tried to explain how subsystems can be brought into consonance with each other. But, although influence flows in both directions, one subsystem usually dominates. This is particularly noticeable when the systems are goal-oriented and are actively striving to influence each other. In such cases it can be interesting to see which of them has most success.

While it is usual in systems theory to regard mapping as a process by which a system's structure is changed in order to adapt to the environment (cf. the quotation from Buckley above), we are also going to examine the opposite process, namely that a system maps its internal structure into the environment. A system's ability to project a mapping of itself into the environment will here be called *dominance*.

Dominance I—Requisite Variety. With his law of 'requisite variety' Ashby (1956) has formulated a major condition for the control of one system by another: the controlling system must have greater variety in its possible 'moves'. To use Ashby's own words: 'Only variety in R can force down the variety due to D: Only variety can destroy variety' (Ashby, 1956, p. 207). We see examples of this everywhere when two complex systems clash in competition. In economic theory price leadership is the best known example of this type of dominance. If competitors know that any measure on their part will call forth a countermeasure from the price leader, and they know that more measures are available to the price leader, then they must accept his dominance. Thus General Motors cannot allow Ford to offer its customers a more varied assortment, because GM would then cease to dominate the market.

> From 1955 to 1960 the partly state-owned Development Company managed to maintain its position as leader of the Swedish atomic energy programme. It had greater variety of resources and could therefore dominate its two challengers, the General Industrial Company and the State Power Board. All three competitors were acutely conscious of the critical role played by this variety. When competition was at its height, both the General Industrial Company and the Power Board tried to persuade the political authorities to curtail the further development of the company; both hoped that certain specialists and experts would then be released and become available to themselves. The idea failed and various attempts at creating 'miniatures' of the Development Company within their own organizations only resulted in their following in its tracks. Every time either of them managed to present any original plans, constructions, or results, the Development Company was always able to quote someone from its own superior network of experts to prove that the suggestions of the other two were impracticable.

Dominance II—Survival of the Fittest. When two or more organized systems interact in a common environment in an ecological system, the organization or the type of organization which is best suited to exploiting the common environment will dominate the others. Dominance can assume a variety of forms. The less well adapted may simply drop out of the environment: companies close down, transfer to other branches of industry or other markets, reduce themselves to the role of subcontractors, or sell out. But since, unlike biological systems, organizations are able to change themselves, other solutions are open to the maladjusted: for instance, the less well adapted organizations often imitate their well-adjusted neighbours. Ford provides a classic example: around 1950 the company adapted its internal structure on the pattern of General Motors, its most formidable rival.

> There are many examples in our material of successful organizations imposing their structure on their competitors in a particular environment. About 50 years ago the Interior Decorating Company started a revolution in its particular branch of industry by cooperating with a bank to introduce a financial innovation. This

soon set the pattern for the industry. Now, as we have described elsewhere, the company is in difficulties. One of the solutions under consideration is to follow the example of a more successful competitor.

Dominance III—Leading Subsystems. In a system consisting of interacting subsystems, which together exploit a common environment or carry out a joint function, some subsystems will often appear more influential than others. In economic theory, Commons (1934) introduced the concept of the limiting or restricting factor. This is the factor, or subsystem, that sets the narrowest limit on the system's total performance. The limiting factor is the weakest link or the bottleneck, to use terms referring to two particular systems. Barnard (1938) uses the expression 'strategic factor' in the same sense.

> If we take any system, or set of conditions, or conglomeration of circumstances existing at a given time, we recognize that it consists of elements, or parts, or factors, which together make up the whole system, set of conditions or circumstances. Now, if we approach this system or set of circumstances, with a view to the accomplishment of a purpose (and only when we so approach it), the elements or parts become distinguished into two classes: those which if absent or changed would accomplish the desired purpose, provided the others remain unchanged; and these others. The first kind are often called limiting factors, the second, complementary factors. ...

> Where the crucial element or part present or absent is a thing or physical element or compound or ingredient it is convenient to call it 'limiting' factor; but when personal or organizational action is the crucial element, *as it ultimately is in all purposive effort,* the word 'strategic' is preferable. (Barnard, 1938, pp. 202–203)

Several organization theorists have presented a similar argument. They have observed that in some companies certain departments or functions are more influential than others and that one will often dominate the others. Consider a company that manufactures staple goods. The ability to produce and distribute articles at a low cost is the decisive competitive factor and the production function naturally carries the greatest weight. On the other hand, in many consumer goods industries, the marketing function dominates. Finally, in the 'innovation' industries, the dominating position may well be occupied by the research and development departments. Emery (1967) uses the term 'the leading part' in a closely related meaning. He discusses the problem of forecasting developments in complex systems, e.g. society. One way of overcoming the unmanageable complexity, he suggests, is to identify subsystems that lead or control others. He refers to McClelland's identification of the 'need for achievement' as a leading part in economic development. In personal discussions with the present author, Emery has given other examples: for more than a century industry has been the leader in social development; now this role seems to have been taken over by higher education, research, and the information and communications system as a whole.

> Selecting the leading part seeks to reduce the total complexity by ignoring a great deal of the specific characteristics of all but one part. At its extremes we have the reduction to a figure-ground relation in which the leading part is considered in relation to all the other parts taken together as its ground (the environment it has which is internal to the total system). Throughout this range of possibilities the method is basically that of establishing which part it is whose goals tend to be subserved by the goals of the other parts or whose goal achievements at t_0 tend to determine the goal achievement of all the parts at t_+. (Emery, 1967, p. 208)

These four mechanisms (mapping, matching, joint consultation and dominance) for achieving consonance between two subsystems are to be understood as simplifications or ideal types. Real life is a great deal more complicated. To begin with, more than two systems are often involved in the change process that leads to consonance. Furthermore, what happens in real life is often a complex mixture of the pure types we have described and defined. And finally, one company may employ quite different mechanisms in adapting to different parts of its environment.

Chapter 3

The Value Environment of the Organization

Examples and Definitions

A lack of consonance between an organization and its environment leads to inefficiency, followed sooner or later by the imposition of sanctions. It is this realization that makes the organization perceive that it has problems.

Although disturbances and variations in the environment are a serious source of problems, structural changes in the environment are what most organizations find hardest to handle. Moreover, as we have seen, of these structural changes the most serious are those involving alteration in norms and values. Here are some examples from various case studies.

> Karl Westlund & Co. is an interesting case. When we first came into contact with the company, it had no problems. Everything seemed to point to excellent adjustment on the part of all those concerned: operations functioned satisfactorily; there was a good grasp of the market; management, customers, etc.—all were happy. The only one who was not entirely contented was the president, who felt that somehow more was required. He came into contact with the outside world more than his colleagues, and he was aware of big changes pending in the industry. He realized that survival was going to call for greater efforts than before. In the course of our work together he became even more dissatisfied. In the end top management split into two camps: one in favour of staying at the company's present base of operations in the north of Sweden; the other infected by the president's dissatisfaction, favouring expansion in the south. In turn the move has spotlighted another problem: in some parts of the environment it is felt that Karl Westlund & Co. is transgressing the norm that says: 'preserve local industry in the north of Sweden'.

> The problem at the Manufacturing Company can be traced back in the main to a breach of the rationality norm. In an economy where rationality demands large-scale production, the company has become a small-scale manufacturer and seller of a great

Table 3:1.   Some examples of value environments

Organization	Evaluator	Evaluative norms, yardsticks	Methods of evaluation
The partly state-owned Development Company	1. Minister of Commerce 2. The group of industries concerned 3. Research community	1. Success in developing independent reactor type 2. Contribution to product development 3. Contribution to research	1. Direct contacts with organization 2. Contact between technical specialists 3. Evaluation of publications
The Registration Office	1. Clients 2. Ministry of Finance	1. Quality of information retrieval 2. Staff increases	1. Informal discussions in client panel 2. Annual budget procedure
The Provincial Savings Bank	1. Public inspector 2. Principals, elected 3. Savings banks association	1. Safety norms 2. Local interests 3. 'Progressiveness'	1. Ratio of retained earnings to total assets 2. Effects of individual decisions on local interest 3. Market share gain through successful participation in new programmes
The Municipal General Hospital	1. Medical profession 2. Local politicians	1. Obedience to professional norms; professional excellence 2. Capacity	1. Informal general evaluation. Formal procedure to evaluate obvious cases of disobedience 2. Statistics of waiting times, staff shortages, number of patients
Employers' Associations	1. Large members (industries)	1a. Contribution to changes in the environment of the industry 1b. Efficiency—low costs	1. Representation on the boards

Organization	Stakeholder	Values	Evaluation/Contact
	2. Small members (handicrafts)	2. Contribution to defence of status quo	2. Contact with local field organizations
	3. Federation of Employers	3. Control of wage increases	3. Efficiency in annual bargaining
Karl Westlund & Co.	1. Clients	1. Prices and support of clients' systems	1. Informal contacts — perceived contribution to solution of clients' problems
	2. The industry	2. Growth, profit, financial stability	2. Informal evaluation of behaviour
The Construction and Building Company	1. Clients	1. Price and reliability	1. Ex-post evaluation of contacts and outcome of joint projects
	2. Owners	2. Profit innovativeness	2. Informal contacts
	3. The industry	3. Growth, profit, financial stability. Conformity with industry norms	3. Informal evaluation of behaviour on the market
The National Rationalization Office (NRO)	Minister of Finance	Reductions in budgets of agencies investigated. Reductions in staff of agencies investigated	Various informal and formal contacts. Personal intuitive overall evaluation
The Transport Administration Office (TAO)	1. Local interest groups	1. Equal treatment for all	1. Public debate, use of political representation
	2. National interest groups	2. Efficiency in transportation subsystems	2. Discussion in various committees, agencies, etc. Public discussion

variety of products. However, it is interesting to note that the immediate and acute problem has arisen from collision with another norm forbidding certain types of restriction on competition. The company is in the domestic appliance business and its chief weapon for combating the harsh competition has been a very efficient sales organization. Particular features have been direct sales to the customer and various services for which a good price has been charged. This is probably going to be forbidden; the company will have to sell its appliances direct to department stores and similar outlets. There will be a drastic drop in profit-earning capacity. A reduction in market share is also feared.

Cooperd is a food company belonging to the Swedish consumers' cooperative. Its difficulties stem mainly from the fact that it is exposed to two irreconcilable norm systems. In the first place the company is judged for its efficiency in supplying the cooperative stores with high-class foodstuffs. Yardsticks are geared to assortment, costs, quality, etc. At the same time, as the cooperative movement has grown and found capital harder to get, it has turned increasingly to the idea of treating every unit as a profit centre expected to provide an adequate yield on invested capital. In this respect Cooperd finds it difficult to obey the norms imposed. The company will have to make some radical changes: restrict its assortment, increase its export, activate its marketing, etc.

In describing the value environment of the organization in more formal terms the following concepts will be used: [13]

Evaluator—a power centre inside or outside the task environment which evaluates the organization in light of a particular norm or yardstick and distributes rewards or punishments accordingly.

Evaluative norms—the norms or yardsticks used by the evaluator. The norms may or may not have been prescribed by the evaluator himself.

Method of evaluation—the procedure used by the evaluator for collecting information, making decisions and feeding back into the organization the outcome of the evaluation.

Table 3 : 1 illustrates some simple examples of value environments.

Characteristics of the Value Environment
That one organization enjoys a relatively problem-free existence while another is dogged by difficulties often depends on differences in the value environments. In a later chapter I will suggest a classification of organizational problems based in part on characteristics of the value environments. Here I will simply mention a few types of differences, with examples based on various case studies.[14]

Environment-oriented and Organization-oriented Norms and Values
Relations between an organization and its task environment are usually
based on some form of voluntary cooperation. The components of the task
environment (grouped according to stakeholder type, for example) assess
the value of their connection with the organization and, if they consider
sanctions necessary, can threaten to withdraw—or actually withdraw—from
further cooperation. This is the 'stakeholder model' of an organization.

But, as we can see in Table 3:1, most organizations are also subject to
some form of general assessment of effectiveness. Thus the Registration
Office was being judged by the Ministry of Finance mainly by its ability to
cut down personnel requirements; when these grew year after year, the
Ministry concluded that the Office was being mismanaged. The Provincial
Savings Bank was being judged by its parent association mainly for

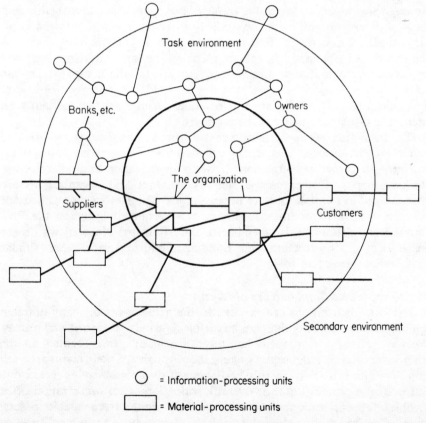

Figure 3:1. The organization, its task environment and its secondary
environment

'progressiveness': was the bank following the various plans prescribed for combating competition from the commercial banks? The Construction and Building Company was being judged by its new owners mainly on a basis of economic yield, but also to some extent for its expansion rate.

The norms and yardsticks of stakeholders are often *environment-oriented*, involving an assessment of organizational performance vis-à-vis the stakeholder and its value or effect. General assessments can follow a similar pattern. For example, the National Rationalization Office (an investigatory body) was assessed by the Minister of Finance according to the budget and personnel savings made in other agencies. But sometimes these general norms and evaluations are oriented more towards the organization itself; they are *organization-oriented*. In other words the organization is assessed according to its internal functioning. In its examination of the Registration Office, the Ministry of Finance increasingly favoured this approach. In the end, the Office was subjected to a very thorough investigation. When the owners investigated the Construction and Building Company, attention was chiefly directed inwards, into the company itself. We can see this from the type of information that was demanded and obtained: i.e. about planning, research, development, and organizational activities to promote the success of the company. On the other hand, so far as we know, the owners made no attempt to discover such things as customer views and reactions. And there was certainly no attempt to assess the quality of the products.

The distinction between environment-oriented and organization-oriented evaluations is far from clear-cut, particularly as many norms and evaluations are concerned with relations between organization and environment. The situation is further complicated by the fact that organizations are often judged in relation to other organizations. The Registration Office, for instance, was being compared with other government agencies, the Provincial Savings Bank with other banks, the Municipal Hospital with other hospitals, the Construction and Building Company with other similar construction firms, and so on.

The Number and Compatibility of Norms

Almost all organizations are exposed to the assessments of many different evaluators—assessments that are based on a variety of norms and values. We have already mentioned that there are many power centres in the environment, each judging the organization in light of their own particular gain from its activities; on this basis reward or punishment is meted out. But even the general (total or overall) evaluation of an organization often involves the application of several, possibly quite irreconcilable, assessments. Changes in the value environment often seem to arise because some long-established set of norms and values, on which the social control of the

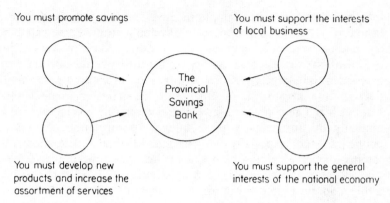

Figure 3:2.   Conflicting norms in the Provincial Savings Bank

organization has been based, meets competition from a new set. At least during a period of transition the organization is then exposed to conflicting evaluations.

For many decades the Registration Office had assumed that its function was to achieve maximum quality, given the prevailing laws and the relevant international agreements. Admittedly there were sometimes clashes in client interests, but it had been possible to solve most of these; an informal council was set up where representatives of the various client groups met the office chiefs at regular intervals and where they could all express their wishes and seek mutually acceptable solutions. The Office was most successful in satisfying the demands of its clients, who generally considered the Office to be one of the foremost service agencies of its type in the world.

However, the straightforward and satisfactory situation was gradually changing; the work load was growing and greater demands were being made on the staff. Moreover, office officials realized that their work was also being assessed by the Ministry of Finance and that norms of another and somewhat conflicting nature were being applied. The Office was being judged by the Ministry for its efforts to improve internal efficiency: to achieve maximum output with a minimum increase in personnel. Wallroth (1968b) has described in detail the problems that faced the Office as a result of this change in value environment.

Some organizations may find themselves in an even more difficult position. The partly state-owned Development Company already mentioned provides an example of this. The company was established for a particular purpose: to develop a reactor type capable of making Sweden independent of the other atomic powers. The organization was assessed each year by the government and the assessment was largely based on information exchanged personally between the organization's chief and the minister immediately responsible. The company was clearly successful; it was rewarded annually by an increase in its budget appropriation. In many countries, and especially in Sweden, President Eisenhower's 'atoms-for-peace' programme had at the same time drawn attention to the potentialities of the atomic industry: it was soon to be a big and profitable business. As minority stakeholders in the Development Company, therefore, various industrial interests demanded a new basis for assessment: the organization should be judged for its contribution to industrial product development. Simultaneously, however, in accordance with another important norm, it was being claimed that state-subsidized companies should not be allowed to compete with the private sector. About ten years later the company was exposed to a further radical change in its value environment. A vociferous group of scientists and politicians wanted the company assessed mainly for its contributions to research. This demand was pushed hard during the debate on budget appropriations. At this stage the situation became so difficult that the Development Company itself called for an investigation into the whole matter and suggested the appointment of a royal commission.

Environment—the Generous and the Restrictive

Some task environments are favourable to the organizations they serve, others less so. In some environments it is virtually impossible to fail; in others difficulties are almost bound to arise. Often, of course, in both the product environment and the raw material and resource environment, this ties up with trends towards expansion or decline.

For many years the Forestry Company has been competing in an industry where admittedly the economic fluctuations had always been severe, but where the company enjoyed an extremely favourable position with access to rich forest resources. For various reasons this situation changed. By the time we were called in, the organization was ready to describe its environment much less favourably: 'Everyone is in difficulties, but we hope to be one of tne last to go under.'

There was one major difference between Karl Westlund & Co. and the Construction and Building Company: the former operated in an environment well supplied with manpower, the latter in a large metropolitan area where it was very difficult, at least at certain times, to maintain an adequate labour force.

That environments can differ in such ways is well known, although not always given sufficient consideration. It is less well known that the value environments of organizations can also vary: some are generous and others restrictive. Most privately-owned companies are ultimately answerable to their owners, who probably base their assessment on the company's economic result.

The case of the Interior Decorating Company provides an interesting example of the big differences that can exist between value environments. The company was one of the largest and, according to many yardsticks, one of the most successful in its line. When we first became involved, the picture was one of undiluted success and smooth running. Management spent much time on improving the homes, schools and social conditions of the already very well organized small local community. At about this time, some changes were made in the board of directors. It was hoped that this would open up new opportunities for contact with other industries and outside experts. It was not long before the new board became aware of some uncomfortable facts: the company's satisfactory financial position depended to a very great extent on its possession of considerable capital and liquid assets; at the same time the yield on this capital had been getting progressively less satisfactory in comparison with what was expected in other industries. Thus, after coming into contact with a broader value environment, the company had become increasingly dissatisfied with itself, and a number of radical changes were decided upon.

Three Types of Value Environment
It should be possible to go some way towards classifying value environments, starting from the distinctions we have just been discussing. However, I must not be too ambitious: my material is incomplete and the organizations and environments studied were not chosen very systematically. Obviously major changes are taking place in organizational environments and these will have to be described more systematically than in the rather superficial attempts at technological forecasting provided by Jantsch (1967), Bell (1967) or Kahn and Wiener (1967). Perrow (1968) has pointed out that Parsons' general social model or Etzioni's system of classification,

for example, could provide fruitful bases for a general analysis of social value environments and the changes they undergo. Kristensson's overall regional model could perhaps be applied to a description in depth of a company's value environment (see Kristensson, 1967). Here we will only distinguish three 'ideal types' of value environment which appear to be particularly interesting, partly because they all have some equivalent in political-economic discussions and partly because they seem able to embrace many of the environmental changes described above. The three value environments reflect to some extent the division into environment-oriented and organization-oriented values that has already been suggested.

Free Value Environments

Characteristic of the *free value environment* is that the supranorms and values are organization-oriented. In the simplest case there will be an assessment of relations with all the stakeholders on the markets; the ultimate yardstick will be company profit. The environment contains a minimum number of norms (prohibitive or prescriptive) all of which are of a very general nature, applying to all organizations. However, this ideal case is rare. In the main the organization is ultimately judged in terms of its own success, although this may not necessarily be equated with profit. Other yardsticks may be size, capital resources, technical elegance, research resources, etc.

Political Environments

Characteristic of the *political environment* is that the ultimate grounds for assessment are environment-oriented. Organizations are evaluated in terms of the effects of their performance on the environment. Various methods can be used. Often the evaluator formulates some sort of plan, budget, or production norm; he then assesses the organization for its success in achieving the chosen objective. The environment usually contains a number of prohibitive and prescriptive norms which, in various ways, regulate what the organization may or may not do. Of the case studies discussed here, the Municipal General Hospital can most nearly be described as having a political environment. The major ground for assessment was the absence of waiting lists for hospital care; obedience to medical norms was strictly controlled.

Mixed Environments

We also need a name for environments that contain both sorts of values (environment- and organization-oriented) and a certain number of prohibitive and prescriptive norms, i.e. environments with features of both the free and the political. For want of anything better, I suggest the term *mixed environment* (in analogy with the mixed economy). This generally means that relations between an organization and its task environment are assessed on a free market, but that other evaluative norms are also applied, subjecting the organization to the demands of a larger system. Some of the values applying in the larger system, such as profit, increase in volume, etc., are organization-oriented; others, such as reputation on the market, contribution to the solving of social problems, etc., are environment-oriented. Among our case studies the most obvious example of an organization working in a mixed environment—and very much aware of the fact—is Karl Westlund & Co. The company operates on the house-building market in northern Sweden. It is judged not only by the usual yardsticks of success in the house-building industry, such as profit and expansion possibilities, but it also has to fulfil certain expectations on the part of the local community, namely to help solve the problems of local employment and education and to engage itself generally in the threatening problems of depopulation.

Growing Importance of the Mixed Environment
Most of the organizations that we studied operate mainly in Sweden or the Scandinavian countries; but in some cases we had reason to make a limited comparison between their environments and others in, for instance, the USA or certain of the communist countries. As is well known from general economic discussion and research, the economic system prevailing in Sweden can be said to possess some features of both a free and a planned economy. Many people believe that this type of mixed economy will become increasingly common.[15] In the course of our investigations we have also made certain comparisons within Scandinavia, for instance between banks, industrial companies, hospitals and government agencies. All this has left us with an impression that in many cases the purely political environments are gradually changing and becoming more mixed. There is a growing tendency to judge the organizations in these environments for their efficiency, success, etc. Attempts are being made to develop new methods of financing and new techniques for measuring performance (e.g. programme budgeting), so that such organization-oriented evaluations will be easier to make. At the same time, companies that have been operating traditionally in free environments now find that they are also being judged by more yardsticks than just profit and success.

Summary—An Example
The Forestry Company operates in a world full of disturbances and variations which cause management a great deal of trouble. Some of the most serious, according to management, are the following:

Fluctuations on the pulp market.

The winters often make lumbering and pulp shipping difficult.

Varying quality of timber.

Supply of timber from outside sources sensitive to competition.

Storm felling upsets lumbering plans.

All through the 1950's and 1960's the company has been trying to improve internal administration, to cope better with the growing problems. Great efforts have been made to improve the tools of forecasting and to combine efficient information systems with decision models of the operations-analysis type. By these means the company has gone a long way towards optimal utilization of its existing forest resources and production system. When we came into the picture, management had just decided to take a major step, combining several of these control systems into one large integrated system for the control of lumbering, transport and production.

At the same time management was becoming increasingly aware that the real threat to the company stemmed not from these disturbances and variations but from a series of structural changes in the environment. These were partly of a kind quite new in the company's experience; moreover it was difficult to get a clear overall picture of them. Some of the most threatening were described as follows:

The company's forest resources were not large enough to support the necessary expansion.

Uneven age structure of mature forests.

Changing structure of forest ownership affects the supply of lumber from outside sources.

Rising wage costs and general difficulties in recruiting forestry workers.

Competition from substitutes—plastics versus cellulose fibre.

When these awkward environmental changes had been sorted out and assessed, management summarized them under three main headings, all of which concerned the value environment of the organization.
1. During the 1950's and 1960's the company had developed at least as favourably as other Scandinavian forestry companies. In the

coming decades this will not be enough. Much more will be needed in the way of efficiency and profit-earning capacity because of greater competition from the USA, the expansion of EEC, and other changes.

2.   The limited supply of company-owned raw materials will force the company to integrate forwards. This will mean a gradual reorganization to meet new types of demands. Efficient production and low costs will not be enough. The company must learn to develop products for the customer. It must become more market-oriented.

3.   After operating for years in a fairly free environment where the main goal was company growth, the organization must now recognize the increasingly political nature of society. If a private enterprise is to survive in a free economy without serious disturbances, it must be prepared to take part in active regional planning, to promote industrial democracy, to work for a better environment, and to pursue various other political goals.

Chapter 4

The Goals of Organizations— Organizations as Means

Value System of the Organization

Since this is the third chapter running (albeit the last) in which I have introduced a number of new concepts, without so far having been able to indicate more than briefly their practical applications, I would like to remind the reader of my aims and the plan of the following argument. My intention in this report is to show how organizational problems arise, and what shapes they can assume; I hope that this will throw some light on how such problems may be solved. I have assumed that the organization is subject to social control. However, as a result of structural changes in the environment, a lack of consonance can easily arise, either between the environment and the organization or between various subsystems and the organization. Sooner or later this leads to sanctions, or at least a threat of sanctions, from some part or parts of the environment: this risk, once perceived, is apprehended as a problem. But environments are not all alike and in the previous chapter I have suggested some simple schemes for describing and characterizing them.

Naturally, if we really want to probe the question of organizational problems, we also need some kind of framework, possibly several, for classifying organizations. The literature is full of suggestions on this point; in Appendix 3 I will discuss the more general problem of describing organizations. Perhaps the most important result of my research into organizational problems, however, is that none of the dimensions usually used for classifying organizations is of central importance when it comes to understanding organizational problems. Neither size, technology nor the administrative set-up is the most important in this context. Instead it appears that an understanding of the value system (often known by the men on the spot as company policy) should provide the basic scheme for anyone trying to discover how organizational problems arise and how they can be solved. The value system is also closely linked to the power system. In the present chapter, on a basis of these findings, I will introduce some concepts which will enable us to describe companies in terms of their value and power systems.

Some Definitions and an Example

The value system of an organization is a system of ideas and attitudes. It embodies the notions of good or bad, of what is desirable or what is not, that govern decision making. The organizational value system has several important functions: it unifies decision making, providing links between decision makers and between decisions made at different times; it also satisfies important psychological needs among members of the organization. Consequently organization members will strive to achieve an inner consistency in the organizational value system and to harmonize their own values with those of the organization. We will call the part of the value system consisting of high-level supra-values the *goal system*.

In his discussion of theory X and theory Y, McGregor (1960) illustrates two interesting examples of such internally consistent value systems. Wallroth (1968a) follows Simon (1947), suggesting that the value systems of organizations are tree-shaped. He also suggests a method of measurement. Stymne (1970) develops this method and illustrates his thesis with examples from three political organizations.[16]

Two Alternative Explanations of Goal Directedness in Organizations

The two functions of the value system—to establish coordination and provide motivation—are not sufficient to explain its hierarchical nature. Value systems tend to constitute a series of means-end sequences, subject ultimately to one or at least comparatively few 'superior' goals. Such goal directedness has often been cited as the special feature that distinguishes organizations from other types of social system (cf. for example Parsons, 1960). If we try to explain goal directedness, and particularly if we try to understand the origins of the 'upper' part of an organizational value system (its goal system), we will find ourselves in one of the most controversial areas of organization theory.

One school claims that the essential goal of organizations (as of living systems) is to ensure their own survival. Barnard (cf. Barnard, 1938) was an early representative of this school. Drucker (1955) has developed the line of reasoning further.

More recent disciples are Katz and Kahn (cf. Katz and Kahn, 1966), who claim that in fact it is unnecessary to speak of goals in describing the environmental adaptation of open systems. Their view has met with opposition, especially from those who emphasize the dominating personal role of management in formulating organizational objectives. Naturally enough practising business leaders are often among these opponents. Fayol (1949) is the classic example. Selznick (1957) also emphasizes the role of the leader. Stymne (1970) has developed Selznick's argument from a starting-point in systems theory.[17]

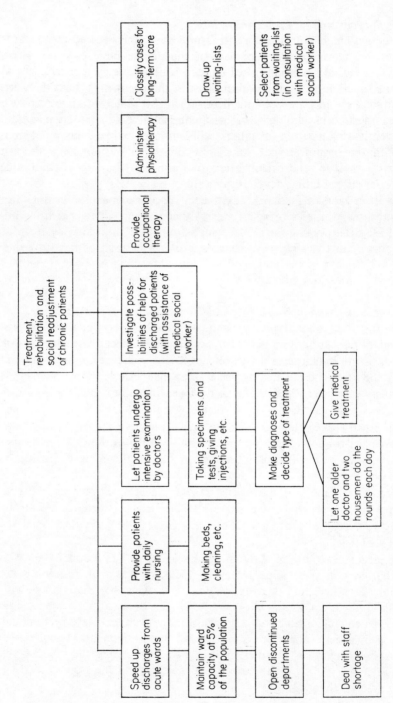

Figure 4:1. The means–end structure of a clinic for chronic patients (Wallroth, 1968a)

An Attempt to Combine the Two Models
Both types of model have their firm supporters and we can point to at least three reasons for the fierceness of the debate between them. First, both sides can call upon empirical data to support their claims. Secondly, the models have been used by both sides in the arguments about the role of profit-maximization in economic theory. Thirdly, the question of organizational goals has been closely connected with political debate on the control of private companies. The fact that empirical data can be cited in support of both theories—the organization as an adaptive open system and the central role of management in goal formulation—naturally encourages us to try to find some explanation to cover both aspects. Various attempts have also been made in the past to combine the two models.

According to the simplest and perhaps most convenient, it is assumed that, in the main, organizations are adaptive in order to survive; further, they are able to adapt because management interprets the demands of the environment and formulates goals accordingly. In an earlier work I have myself used this explanation (Rhenman, 1968a).

Cyert and March (1963) do not explicitly discuss this problem. However, they indicate the possibility of a combination of the two models: they assume that goal formulation goes through several phases and that the role of management varies accordingly. In a first coalition phase the greatest need is for negotiators and mediators. In a later stabilization phase management has to design tools of administrative control and to operationalize and specify company goals. In a third adaptive phase the demands of the environment and the situation of the organization must be watched and negotiations with stakeholders perhaps renewed.

Galbraith (1967) develops an argument that many others had previously touched upon. We can combine the two models of organizational goal formulation if we accept that the quest for survival implies certain minimum goals (restrictions). Once these goals have been fulfilled greater freedom of action becomes possible. Not only management but also many other high-level officials and experts are also involved in formulating the goals. The personal interests of these persons are the chief determining factor.

We have found Galbraith's approach best suited to explain the experiences we gained from our case studies. I have extended Galbraith's argument somewhat to allow for the very considerable differences that exist between organizations, particularly in the nature of their goals and the degree of organizational independence.

Goals as a Base for Classifying Organizations
According to the definition suggested above, the goals of an organization consist of the 'superior' values that obtain. Let us further suppose that

these have been formally stated. For the time being we can forget that it is not always easy to get the goals prescribed in a company to accord with the prevailing value system. Nor need we concern ourselves with a question that interests many researchers, namely: who formulates the goals? We can simply assume that, in some organizations at least, there is some person or persons who prescribes goals and who is able, by means of the power he wields or in some other way, to get these goals realized, i.e. accepted as the basis of the organization's system of values.

I will employ the following concepts:

The *organizational role* is a description of (a) the environmental elements (possibly combined into stakeholder groups) with which the organization has exchange relations, (b) these exchange relations, and (c) the power relations with each stakeholder.

Organizational resources include the technical, economic and personnel resources of the organization.

The role and resources of an organization at a particular time describe its *strategic position.* Barnard (1938) was probably the first organization theorist to consider the strategic position. I have provided an example of this elsewhere, in a description of a Swedish general hospital (Rhenman, 1969).

Internal or *strategic goals* are ideas about desirable future strategic positions. *Strategy* or *strategic plan* are ideas about how the internal goals are to be attained. The person or persons inside or outside the organization who originates these ideas is described as the *strategic management* of the organization.

Ansoff (1965) is one of the best known writers to have studied strategic planning and strategic management. He is particularly interested in strategic goals that imply growth. I do not feel able at present to publish any of the strategic plans which I have seen formulated in various Scandinavian companies. Instead I have chosen what seems a typical example from the literature.

1. Increase manpower by 15 per cent in X years,
2. Improve production efficiency so that total corporate growth exceeds 15 per cent,
3. Seek and develop products and markets to utilize the projected manpower growth,
4. Utilize existing technology in product development to the extent possible, instead of seeking new knowledge through investment in basic research,
5. Continue business activities with the present type of products, but be alert for opportunities to diversify and make acquisitions or other investments, and

6. Provide the necessary financing for the preceding strategic plans. (From the book, *Long-Range Planning Practices in 45 Industrial Companies*, p. 56, by H. W. Henry. © 1967 by Prentice-Hall, Inc., Englewood Cliffs, N.J., U.S.A., and used with their permission)

External or *institutional goals* (sometimes also called the *mission* of the organization) are ideas about the effects of organizational operations on the environment. The originator of these ideas or stipulations is described as the *institutional management* of the organization.

> The Provincial Savings Bank which we have already described can provide an example. It had three external or institutional goals: to encourage savings, to provide its customers with security, and to promote local interests.

We can now consider four types of organization as illustrated in Figure 4:2 below. Our classification has been drawn up so as to allow for the existence of internal and/or external goals and the presence or absence of strategic or institutional managements.

Organizations...	...without strategic or internal goals, therefore no strategic management	...with strategic or internal goals and a strategic management to formulate them
...without institutional or external goals, therefore no institutional management	'MARGINAL ORGANIZATIONS'	'CORPORATIONS'
...with institutional or external goals and an institutional management to formulate them	'APPENDIX ORGANIZATIONS'	'INSTITUTIONS'

Figure 4:2. Four types of organization

As I will show in Chapter 5, I do not expect the organizations of real life to fall neatly within these four boxes. The diagram simply represents the end-points of scales or, more succinctly, 'ideal types'.

Some Examples of Organizational Goals

The four types of organization defined in the previous section can now be briefly exemplified. My aim is simply to familiarize the reader with the concepts which will be used later, for instance in examining the types of environment which offer the best chance of success to the different classes of organization, or the way in which organizations develop.

Marginal Organizations. According to our definition, the marginal organization lacks both strategic and institutional goals. Of course this does not necessarily mean that the strategic position of the organization is fixed once and for all. But the strategic changes do not follow any pre-scribed plan. Classical economic theory assumes all organizations to be marginal. As we shall see later, under certain conditions marginal organizations can be very successful.

Among our case studies interesting examples of marginal organizations were provided by a group of publishing firms in southern Sweden. Six of them satisfied our definition and most of these six also showed the highest profits. As organizations they were all very small. A couple of them were prepared to abandon publishing at any time if some other golden oppor-tunity arose.

But marginal organizations are not necessarily small. A Finnish com-pany that we studied employed almost a thousand people; it still had neither external nor internal goals. However, this is fairly unusual. For reasons that will be discussed later, it so happens that marginal organiza-tions usually come under a strategic management after reaching a certain size. This management begins to formulate internal goals so that the company becomes, according to our definition, a corporation.

Corporations. This type of organization has a strategic management which has formulated strategic (internal) but not institutional goals. Organizations with strategic goals often have strategies too. The nature of the strategic goals and of the strategy will depend to a great extent on the environment and on changes in the environment.

Up to now business organization theorists and related writers on long-range planning have concentrated almost exclusively on corporations. We found in our case studies that the objectives of corporations are generally as Ansoff (1965) and others have described them, i.e. including goals and plans for increased return on investment, product diversification, rationali-zation, profit improvements, etc.

Appendix Organizations. The appendix organization has an institutional management but no strategic management. It operates for the purposes of outside interests; its own advancement is of less concern. Survival is not an end in itself. There has been very little discussion of the goal problems of appendix organizations in organization literature.

If we were to limit our investigations to the large industrial companies, we would not come across many appendix organizations. On the other hand it is quite common for an appendix organization to emerge as an 'offshoot' of another organization (the parent). The parent establishes the appendix for a specific purpose. When this has been fulfilled or becomes obsolete, the implication is that the appendix may be dissolved or trans-formed. This may even be openly stated. The same applies if the appendix proves unsuited to its appointed task. Government agencies, voluntary organizations, the subsidiaries of large industrial companies (e.g. sales companies) can all belong to this category. The institutional management is usually to be found in the parent organization.

The Municipal General Hospital that we studied proved to be an appendix organization; its parent, containing the strategic management, was the county council. The hospital had a management of its own (the Hospital Board), but this formulated neither strategic nor institutional goals. Instead its sole concern was day-to-day administration and immediate problems.

The Registration Office, a government agency, regarded itself as an appendix organization; despite pressure from a group of its own middle-managers, top management refused to formulate either strategic or institutional goals. Working within the framework of its external goals (instructions from the Ministry), the Office tried year after year to adjust to changes in the environment. Serious problems ultimately arose because its principal was not able to make sufficient change or adjustment in the external goals.

Institutions. Institutions have both strategic and institutional goals. The strategic management may or may not be identical with the institutional management. This question will be discussed below. I will also examine the interesting conflicts that can arise between the two managements. As in the case of the appendix organization, institutional management may be found outside the organization, whereas the strategic management is always located inside. The institution has been best described by Selznick (1949 and 1957). I have already mentioned that his interpretation of *role* and *mission* agrees more or less with that used here.

Of the organizations that we studied, the Transport Administration Office (TAO) is perhaps the most typical institution. Strategic and institutional management are combined under a director general. The interesting point here is that this combination has come about as the result of a gradual liberation from the government department which was previously responsible for formulating goals. The institutional goals were in the nature of a 'vision' of the desired future state of the transport system. At the same time they had been partly codified in a written plan. The director general and his colleagues found it more difficult to find time to deal with the strategic goals, but a long-range plan gradually emerged.

Goals at Different Stages of Organizational Development

Michels' study of trade unions (1911) was probably the first empirical work to show how organizational goals tend to change as organizations develop (Michels, 1962). This has since been widely discussed. A survey of the literature was made by Sills (1957). Among other things it appears that organizations can change products and/or clients; that a means can gradually become an end in itself; that survival emerges as an important goal; and that the environment (clients, colleagues, opponents, etc.) affect organizational goals. Earlier writings on the subject, and our case studies, are summarized in Figure 4:3 below. Some comments follow the figure.

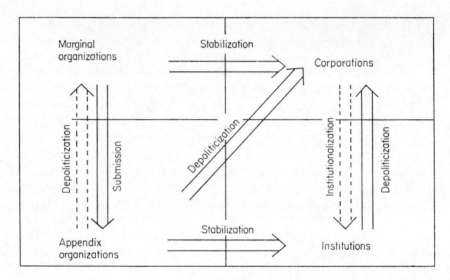

Figure 4:3.   Goals at different stages of development

Newly Established Organizations

Organizations are established either as appendix organizations or as marginal organizations. In the first case a unit from outside (e.g. another organization) creates the new organization with a definite goal in view.

Government agencies are a typical example. The term *agency* indicates that the organization exists to carry out the goals of another. Marginal organizations are often established because a person or persons, having some resources available, sees a possibly temporary opportunity, for instance a need on the market, of putting the resources to profitable use. The typical small entrepreneur starts his company as a marginal organization, without any further plan then 'to try and see what happens'.

Dissolution or Subjection

Many appendix and marginal organizations continue as they began. But, although they may stay the same for a very long time, it is in fact remarkable how many organizations do change their character over the years. When an appendix organization has attained its goal, or is judged by the parent organization as being inadequate for its purpose, it may be dissolved. When a marginal organization fails to find any fresh opportunity for development, it is generally sold by its owners to a larger company, or declared bankrupt.

If the marginal organization is sold to a larger company, it may function as an appendix organization, serving a particular purpose of the parent company. Or the marginal organization may subject itself to a larger organization as a subcontractor or agent, often within the terms of a long-term contract.

Stabilization

Another common development in the marginal or appendix organization is the emergence of an internal strategic management which regards the survival or growth of the organization as an end in itself. What we have called a process of *stabilization* sets in. The stabilization of the marginal organization often seems to coincide with the passing of a management generation: perhaps the founder and boss, whose main gift was his nose for business and his flair for grasping the golden opportunity, disappears; he is replaced by an employed official, to whom the formulation of strategic goals often appears as a necessity.

Depoliticization

An appendix organization in competition with independent companies is often frustrated by its dependence on a principal, and its obligation to serve the principal's ends. The appendix feels hampered and inefficient; it wants to be free.

> An industrial company found that after several years its service workshop had developed into an independent company which was increasingly uninterested in granting any special privileges to the parent company. An air company, founded originally by two newspaper concerns to distribute newspapers and transport passengers, soon found it necessary to shift the balance very much to the disadvantage of the newspaper-distribution interests. Otherwise it would not have been possible to develop healthily on the market for passenger transport.

An institution in competition with independent corporations may also find its external goals inhibiting. I will call the processes by which organizations seek to deal with such situations *depoliticization*.

Institutionalization

A marginal organization which develops into a corporation, i.e. which has drawn up goals for its own development and which possesses resources with which to realize them, will sometimes reach institution status. This may be the unplanned result of, for example, a selective recruitment policy, perhaps geared to the local manpower situation or to the solution of other social problems. In other cases it may result from cooperation with institutions which already have certain external goals. Shared responsibility for these may be the price of other desired advantages. Selznick (1957) has called processes of this sort *institutionalization*.

Quasi-institutionalization has been described by Galbraith and others. It reveals itself in at least three ways:

1. A tendency to change strategic goals into ends in their own right— quasi-institutional goals. According to Galbraith, growth and technical virtuosity are quasi-institutional goals. Later I will provide some more examples.
2. A tendency to formulate fancy goals that don't really mean a thing. Galbraith is worth quoting here too:

    > Building a better community; improved education; better understanding of the free enterprise system; an effective attack on heart ailments, emphysema, alcoholism, hard chancre or other crippling disease; participation in the political party of choice; and renewed emphasis on regular religious observances are all examples of such further goals. (Galbraith, 1967, p. 176)

3. Surplus of resources is concealed in 'slack', instead of being directed towards institutional goals. (Cf. Cyert and March, 1963)

Some Observations

In our case studies we found depoliticization to be much more usual than institutionalization. In this respect our experience differs from Selznick's. Perhaps this can be explained by the following general trends in the environment.

De-ideologization in society and value relativism result in the depoliticization of organizations. New external goals tend to appear in the shape of aids to strategic planning. Institutional goals no longer dominate strategic goals; instead they are seen as a means towards the survival of the organization. A typical example is provided by the sort of discussion about goals sometimes heard in religious or other popular organizations: the problem is seen as one of developing new saleable products. A business leader made the following comment on the Swedish state church.

> The surprising thing to an ordinary simple consumer of Christian information—and most of us are still just that—is that the retreat of the Church has taken place without those responsible ever, so far as I know or have heard, seeing the problem for what it is; *a question of marketing.*

> Which of the services performed by the Church really attract a public about to enter the 1970's? I do not know, and I wonder whether the question has ever been seriously asked by the Church. Until you know what services you have to sell, and how the public will react to your products, you should be very cautious about your investment in advertising. Otherwise you may well risk a poor investment. (Elinder, 1966, pp. 4–5) (Our translation)

Growing competition and far-reaching environmental change make it difficult to cope with a conflict between institutional and strategic goals. As a consultant to a big consumers' cooperative organization has put it: 'You must solve your business problems before starting to improve society.' Markets are growing, which means that the average size of organizations is increasing to match. The advantages of scale are essentially on the marketing side, where the need for strategy is also greatest. Increasing size is accompanied by a techno-structure where growth becomes an end in itself. Finally it seems to me significant that so little is known about institutional leadership. The subject has rarely been discussed; few opportunities for training exist. The institutional leader is apparently expected to rely on his natural gifts. And yet very special methods are required for realizing institutional goals (e.g. selective recruitment). Lastly—and this perhaps explains the absence of discussion and training—it is doubtful whether institutional leadership is regarded as a legitimate task for business leaders in our society. 'Companies are for meeting market demand, not for pursuing politics.'

Value-supportive Systems
It is not enough for the goals of a large organization to be formulated and its values prescribed by the strategic or institutional management. If the goals are to be achieved and the values applied, they will have to permeate all action and all decision making throughout the organization. Selznick (1957) talks about the task of embodying the goals and values of the organization in the social structure. This is a vivid description of something that we have also noticed: in any organization where decision

making is decentralized much more will be needed than, say, a codified company policy expressing management's values. The values that will actually affect company behaviour will depend on other more concrete systems.

The Power and Status System

Values which can be backed by power and/or status (these two systems are of course interdependent) are more likely to influence day-to-day decision making than values lacking such support. The backing may come from inside or outside the organization; if from outside, its source may be other cooperating organizations, clients, consultants or evaluators. The value system of the organization will be decisively affected by the composition of the board, the formal organization, and the system of rewards, all of which operate through the power and status system.

Thus, the greater the power and status of management, the greater the chance that management can impose prescribed goals on the prevailing value system. If other power centres inside or outside the organization are recognized by members as representing other values, management will be in some difficulty. Any parts of the organization whose sole contact is with such non-management status centres or power centres will be particularly hard to influence.

> In some ways, the workers employed by the Construction and Building Company came into closer contact with the trade union than with the company, and in so far as the union appeared to have more power to create continuous employment, management found it difficult in some respects to influence its employees.

> At the Provincial Savings Bank some officials were in daily contact with customers. They tended to be affected by customer values and showed considerable resistance to certain management goals. For instance, they were unwilling to follow instructions on the restriction of certain types of loan.

> The most marked example noted by us, in which the grass roots of an organization were influenced more by the local environment than by the prescribed goals of management, was the regional organization of the Federation of Employers. Stymne (1970) has reported that this organization often worked for objectives in direct opposition to the prescribed goals of central management.

> The Development Company provides an example of the successful use of power and status to support prescribed goals. In this

instance it was possible in a relatively short time to change a pure research organization into a development and construction company that was at least in part successful. The chief weapon in achieving this was the placing of a person representing the new values in the most powerful position in the company; at the same time the person who had previously most strongly supported research left the organization.

The System of Symbols

The language used in an organization is a powerful weapon: it colours the perceptions of organization members, affecting the decisions they make. We came across many examples of leaders systematically using value-laden words (sometimes even slogans) to steer the ambitions of their organizations in the 'right' direction. Symbols, rites and other forms of value-worship can also be used to give values a greater direct impact.

In Inmec the leader had launched the idea of the 'technological gap', to underscore the importance of product development. The expression refers to the company's difficulty in keeping up with the rate of technological development exhibited by its American and Japanese competitors.

In the Provincial Savings Bank and in the cooperative service firms there was a fully developed ideology based mainly on the conditions of several decades ago, when the companies were founded. This ideology described the community, the company, opponents and customers. A number of terms such as 'the savings bank tradition', 'the common good', 'the wellbeing of society', 'local prosperity', etc. had a meaning only for those who had made themselves familiar with the whole ideology (see also Hellgren and Wirenhed, 1968)

The most common types of symbol in organizations are historical persons or events, and enemies. Practically every one of the organization which we studied had known at least one critical experience, the memory of which was still preserved and for which various symbols existed.

The Development Company had what amounted to an internal calendar with two eras—'before' and 'after' The Conflict. This referred to a conflict with a large privately-owned company. The names of certain persons who had taken part in these events were still strongly emotive, although many of the present employees could never have known them personally.

The Employers' Federation had preserved the thirty-year-old memory of a conflict with the workers. The regional organization had developed a special language for describing their 'enemies'.

Karl Westlund & Co. and the Construction and Building Company had each at some time faced serious liquidity crises; in both companies veterans of the crisis formed an élite who, particularly on social occasions, dug up their 'war' memories for a thorough airing.

Other Value-supportive Systems

Since people enter the organization armed with a battery of personal values which they then try to realize there, the organization's value system can be affected by recruitment, retirements or internal transfers.

For the partly state-owned Development Company the move to a small town without a university proved fateful. Admittedly most of the staff transferred to the new plant, but during the years just before and just after the move to the new research station, a number of leading researchers left to join various universities. If the company had instead moved to a university town it would probably have been easier to preserve values geared more closely to research and academicism.

If a decision is to be used to support a value or a change in a value, it must first be possible for management to enforce it. It is easier to impose a change in physical conditions than social conditions; and it is easier to sway observable than non-observable behaviour.

Changes in the external goals of the Provincial Savings Bank, especially those concerned with the safeguarding of local interests, were embodied in a decision about establishing and closing down new branches. Two values were in conflict: on the one hand was the pure profit and efficiency motive, according to which any branch office that did not contribute to company profits should be closed down, and on the other the traditional attitude that the local community should be preserved at all costs (the very community to which the bank owed its birth). Management was split when it came to the exact interpretation of this second value. Both sides had difficulty in expressing their views concretely and fell back on a simple enumeration of the branch offices that should be closed down. It was also interesting to listen to the arguments between the profit-motive supporters and those in favour of preserving the social goals. The latter group dressed up most of their arguments in economic terms; they questioned the profit estimates, suggesting that certain branch revenues were difficult to assess and that various interdependencies between branch offices, etc. should be taken into account.

Changes in procedures or administrative systems can influence behaviour in organizations in two ways: either directly, by changing the problem-solving ability (the cognitive system), or indirectly through the value system. Before I embarked on this project I was pretty ignorant of the sometimes highly value-laden nature of certain administrative techniques.

As consultants to the Registration Office we found ourselves supporting the disciples of a simplified and rationalized product procedure. By suggesting a system of efficiency budgeting, we provided this faction with a decisive weapon. The director general decreed that every organizational unit must estimate their intended percentage productivity increase for the coming period; they were also to produce a list of projected rationalization measures. It was then much more difficult for the other camp (those who claimed that the problems of the Office were all a question of resources: 'the Minister of Finance is responsible for the long delay in handling requests from clients') to withstand the demand for change.

Network planning (Pert) affected conditions in the partly state-owned Development Company in a similar way. Since it was now possible to trace the cause of delays and pin the responsibility on the person or persons concerned, a new norm could be applied: 'deadlines must be kept!' It is doubtful, however, whether the result was an improvement in total efficiency, or whether resources were simply transferred from general research to Pert-planned projects.

The Individual and the Goals of the Organization
Disagreement between prescribed goals and the values on which decision making and action in organizations is based, is one of the main problems discussed by psychologists interested in organization theory. The starting-point is almost always the existence of a conflict between individual and organizational goals. The individual feels threatened. His motivation is weak. He does not have sufficient chance to develop his potentialities. (Cf. Mayo, 1967; McGregor, 1960; Argyris, 1965 and others.) There is no

doubt that this is a frequent reaction, and one that will be discussed below. But it will also be seen that the same problem can be viewed from quite another angle.

The Political System and Other Defence Systems

Any disagreement between organizational and individual values will be experienced as a threat by the individual concerned. He will want to protect himself against the values conflicting with his own. Similarly, changes in the value-supportive systems will sometimes be felt as a threat, invoking special systems of defence.

Two defence systems are of particular interest: the ideological and the political. Certain types of ideology help people to accept a simplified or distorted picture of causal complexities; it can thereby make incompatible values appear compatible. As Sutton *et al.* (1956) has shown, managements often launch a special 'management ideology' to make their dictatorial role appear compatible with 'democracy'.

In the political system, people work together to support values that appear to be threatened. Political systems are sometimes formal, embodied for example in trade unions; sometimes they are informal. Dalton (1959) and Burns (1961) have described political systems in organizations: such systems often contain 'parties' corresponding to the formal departments in the organization. In much the same way people with similar educational backgrounds (engineers, doctors, lawyers, economists, nurses, etc.) often seem to form political groups in organizations; age groups show similar tendencies. Later I will report several of my own observations, showing the strength of such political systems of defence.

'We Want Clearer Goals'

Unavoidable conflicts are not the only obstacle to achieving consonance between organizational and employee goals. In our case studies we often found people in subordinate positions complaining over the absence of leadership, or of clear-cut goals imposed from above.

> I have been head of some pretty big units in a couple of large American companies. It was just the same in both of them. It was never difficult to discuss investments, storage problems, new computer equipment or personnel problems with management. But as soon as I tried to start some discussions of goals and strategy—nothing doing! They left that to me. What really should have been their job.

This quotation is from an interview with an American business leader, but we frequently heard similar declarations from members of the partly state-owned Development Company, the Provincial Savings Bank, the Forestry Company and the Construction and Building Company. In fact a closer look at our records reveals that we heard the same type of complaint whenever we managed to make close contact with the employees at levels below the managerial. It should be noted, however, that the complaints were not directed towards the particular goals or policy of the company; the point was that employees wished management would devote more attention to these problems and would make their opinions better known.

In the International Corporation complaints were even heard among the members of top management; it was felt that the president should give a far more clear-cut idea of what he was trying to do and that top management should have more say in the formulation of goals. One respondent told us: When it comes to long-range planning, relations between top management and the various divisions are not what they should be. In fact it seems to me that the President has been alone in formulating the company's overall strategy. Even in top management we have had no active part in it—he's more or less decided it all himself.

Almost as often we found that top management's ideas about the value system of its own organization were extremely vague, if not actually wrong.

The management of the Development Company saw as the most characteristic feature of the organization its ability to carry out large projects (project orientation). In fact there was little foundation for this view; later events revealed that the truth was almost the opposite. In its own eyes the Provincial Savings Bank was very service-minded, although our investigation revealed that the organization was, characteristically, almost totally ignorant of the desires of its customers. Members of the Registration Office would have said that their organization was geared to the needs of the economy and of industry, although top management's chief contact was with similar organizations in other countries.

This unawareness of the organizational value system is sometimes coupled with a lack of insight into the effects of certain decisions on the system. Another case with which we came in contact concerned a cooperative service company which was considering an agreement for closer cooperation with a political organization. One of the major effects was likely to be a change in the actual operations of the company in, as it seemed to the customers, a definitely new political direction. Of course management may have been aware of this probability; perhaps those who supported the suggestion were trying to politicize the company. However, in the discussions to which we were invited, and in our interviews with board members and various managers, these effects on the value system were either ignored altogether or only mentioned in passing. This experience agrees very closely with the interpretation in Selznick (1957).

> When institutional leadership fails, it is perhaps more often by default than by positive error or sin. Leadership is lacking. . . .
> In statemanship no less than in the search for personal wisdom, the Socratic dictum . . .—know thyself—provides the ultimate guide.
> (Selznick, *Leadership in Administration*, Harper and Row, Inc., 1957, pp. 25–26)

Organization Character—An Example

As I have already intimated, Selznick is the organization theorist who has most influenced my attempts to understand organizations. Following his example, I have carried out intensive case studies together with my colleagues, in which I have also taken into account the historical development of the organizations concerned. For me, then, Selznick's concept of organization character is one of the most interesting in organization theory. At the same time it is not at all an easy concept to grasp, partly because Selznick never defines it except by comparing it with the psychological concept of personality. Even then, as he points out, the psychological concept itself is not altogether clear. In his opinion, however, there is agreement on four points :

> First, character is a *historical* product. 'The character as a whole', writes Fenichel, 'reflects the individual's historical development'. Character is the 'ego's habitual ways of reacting'. In this sense every individual has a unique character.

> Second, character is in some sense an *integrated* product, as is suggested by the term 'character-structure'. There is a discoverable pattern in the way the ego is organized; and the existence of such a pattern is the basis of character analysis.

> Third, character is *functional,* in the sense that it is no mere accidental accretion of responsible patterns. Character develop-

ment fulfills a task set by the requirements of personality organization: the defense of the individual against inner and outer demands which threaten him. . . .

Fourth, character is *dynamic,* in that it generates new strivings, new needs and problems. It is largely through the identification of these needs that diagnosis proceeds, as when the discovery of excessive dependency or aggressiveness suggests that the patient has a particular type of character-structure.
(Selznick, *Leadership in Administration,* Harper and Row, Inc., 1957, pp. 38–39)

In a way this chapter represents an attempt to operationalize the concept of organization character. With the frame of reference given here it could be defined as a system of systems, in other words the system of the organization's value system and its value-supportive systems. It is also interesting to try to see how this character has developed historically in interaction with the environment. An example from an earlier report can illustrate my theoretical approach (Rhenman and Wallis, 1967).

Since its establishment three values had always guided the efforts of management members in the Provincial Savings Bank. They wanted to encourage saving. They wanted to give their customers security. And they wanted to promote the interests of the local community. Other credit institutions, e.g. the general savings banks, gave official expression to similar values. But for the Provincial Savings Bank, and for many other savings banks, these three values were more than empty phrases. The Bank's history contains many interesting examples of how it supported (or, to use Selznick's term, embodied) these values. The encouragement of saving, for example, was embodied in what was probably one of the first sales organizations in Sweden: a network of offices opened in all the grade schools in the county and run voluntarily by teachers and other officials. The provision of security was in part embodied in the investment policy. The bank abstained from various apparently profitable investments—investments that brought profit to many commercial banks at the beginning of the century but which, risky as they were, later brought ruin. Security was also embodied in the internal organization where certain rules charged the board with direct responsibility for the day-to-day business of the bank. The promotion of local interests was embodied mainly in the trustee organization. Ultimately responsible for the running of the bank were 50 trustees, all of whom were well known and respected in the community. Later the rules for the appointment of trustees were changed; half of them were to be appointed direct by the local authorities.

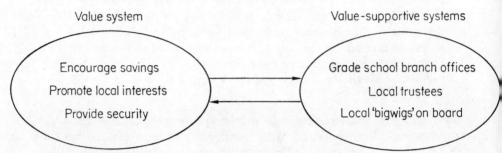

Figure 4:4.   Character of the Provincial Savings Bank

This example also shows how an interest in the organization's value system makes the analysis dynamic. Lodged in its system of values is the organization's heritage from its past. It is these values which, more than anything else, determine what the organization can or cannot do in the future.

Chapter 5

Problems of Structural Change

We can now continue our analysis of organizational adaptation to structural changes in the environment. We can combine the environmental and organizational models suggested in Chapters 3 and 4 with the ideas about how efficiency is achieved suggested in Chapter 2. I will also try to generalize from my own and my colleagues experience of organizations, in order to analyse the problems that arise in connection with structural change. Naturally environments and organizations do not exist in the pure forms postulated here; nevertheless I will continue to use these ideal cases as analytical models. That real companies and business leaders are often faced with a combination of the problems and difficulties described below is an unavoidable complication. I will return to it in the summary at the end of this chapter.

Different Types of Organization in Different Value Environments

It appears, as has already been mentioned, that the most serious organizational problems arise from dissonance between the oragnization's value environment and its own value system, and the consequent drop in external efficiency. I will now examine some examples of each of the four types of organization.

Marginal Organizations and Corporations

The value systems of the marginal organization and the corporation harmonize best with the values of a free value environment. The marginal organization and the corporation are generally to be found on markets and seldom in a controlled economy. In a political environment both run serious risks of landing in difficulties. They will be regarded with great mistrust and probably subjected to strict regulation and control. The marginal organization runs the risk of incorporation into some more trusted institution as an appendix, and the corporation will be coerced towards institutionalization. They will frequently prove unable to make adequate contribution to the function of the superior system. In Sweden where the social and medical systems are becoming embraced by a political environment, an example is provided by the pharmaceutical industry. Despite remarkable internal success and despite its considerable contribution to the function of Swedish society, the industry is being exposed to increasingly strict controls (which, incidentally, are creating serious problems for the companies concerned). In the long run the industry runs the risk of socialization.

In our case material the building industry provides the best illustration of the difficulties of the marginal organization or the corporation in a political environment. In its post-war programme, the Swedish Social Democrat Party set a number of political goals for the provision of housing. The party has been in power ever since and has enjoyed the possibility of cooperation with the trade unions; it has thus had plenty of opportunity for realizing its goals. The Swedish building industry could therefore be described as existing in a fairly typical political environment, at least until the middle of the 1960's. At that point a certain amount of freedom began to be introduced in a conscious attempt to create what could be called in our terminology a mixed environment. The political goals included an increase in the standard of housing, keeping prices down, using the industry to regulate economic fluctuations, and the reduction of seasonal variations in the employment of labour. The government did not feel that the private building industry or the independent builders were best fitted to realize these goals. It seemed doubtful that the industry would be able to keep prices down and so price control was introduced. It was also felt that the regular employment of labour was not always sufficiently considered and various steps were taken to guarantee better conditions, etc. The result has been that during the post-war period the private builders (marginal organizations and corporations) have lost a large share of the market for new housing. The trade union movement has established what is now by far the largest company for the building of houses and several municipal and cooperative building societies have gone into production on their own.

Even in a mixed environment marginal organizations and corporations will find that their own values do not always accord with those of the environment and this is likely to cause difficulties. The best example from our material is provided by the conflict described above between the Manufacturing Company and society. The company tried to dominate a particular market for domestic appliances by selling direct to consumers.

Appendix Organizations
The value system of an appendix organization is best adapted to the

political value environment. As we have already seen, the appendix organization is usually to be found in special environments where it is dominated by some other large organization (the state or a corporation) and used for the latter's purposes. In a planned economy or in a limited sphere under state domination, any organization that fails to subordinate itself to the prevailing political goals, i.e. which does not accept its position as an appendix of the large system, will be in difficulties.

It has been pointed out above that there are certain mechanisms which appear to set the appendix organization on a course away from the political and towards the free environment. Perhaps there is a conscious or unconscious desire to free the organization from its principal; or perhaps surplus resources are available. For either of these reasons attempts may be made to establish the organization on a free market. Numerous examples can be found of the resulting difficulties, all of which have a specific source: the organization, whose whole value system is geared to external goals, is not adaptable like the marginal organization and cannot choose and dominate its environment like the corporation. Two examples:

The partly state-owned Development Company was founded as an appendix organization of the Ministry of Commerce and given fixed external goals. When these goals subsequently lost much of their importance the company was threatened with a considerable reduction in operations. It tried to free itself from the Ministry and stabilize its situation by setting up as a research institute and seeking research contracts. All directors of research were enjoined to 'sell' their services. There was much discussion about establishing a marketing department and half-hearted efforts in that direction were made. One director who happened temporarily to be free was appointed sales manager. Naturally his standing was far removed from that of a sales director in a corporation. A few contracts were sold, generally at a loss, and several years later operations were still on a very small scale. A major customer relates: 'I visited their research station but I soon realized that no one there knew how to tackle goal-oriented projects. They were used to research as a sort of continuous operation; they'd no idea how to develop products or new systems.' This judgment may not be entirely just but can serve to reflect the impression of an onlooker.

The Service Company owned by Charter Aircraft had been started to provide airborne meals and to operate restaurants at certain traffic centres under the company's domination. Subsequently the firm took over a couple of other restaurant businesses, thus gaining possession of some restaurants outside the original traffic centres. For this reason and because of overcapacity in its kitchens, the Service Company was in a position to sell its services on the open restaurant market. From the start profits were poor; the firm was known for running some of the worst restaurants in the business. On the open market the expected standard of service and prices was quite different from that required by the parent company; for them the main criteria were reliable deliveries and great flexibility. Moreover it was difficult for the firm to get from the parent company the resources necessary for developing its new operations.

Institutions

The institution is best fitted to succeed in a mixed environment. It has internal goals which give it the advantage over the appendix organization; it also has external goals and is therefore less likely than the corporation to get into political difficulties with its environment. This combination of internal and external goals accords well with the demands of the environment: the organization is expected to be successful and to contribute to the function of the superior system.

If the external goals are satisfactorily embodied in the organization and at the same time correspond to important social needs, the institution may, as Selznick (1957) has pointed out, acquire a distinctive competence. Figure 5:1 illustrates this possibility (see also the description of the Provincial Savings Bank at the end of Chapter 4).

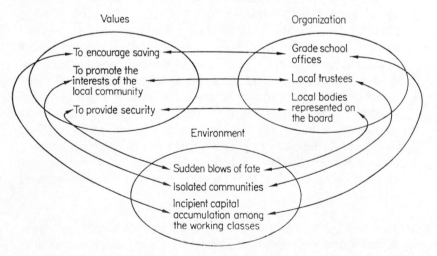

Figure 5:1.   Distinctive competence of the Provincial Savings Bank

On the other hand institutions can be expected to get into difficulties in a free or a political environment. In the former they will find it difficult to hold their own vis-à-vis the corporations which, in that environment, will be more efficient than they are themselves. And in the political environment the institution will often conflict with the demands of the environment because of the need to weigh internal and external goals against each other. Examples can be found of both types of problem.

> Cooperative Services provides an interesting example of an institution's difficulties in competing with a corporation. CS had grown up in a mixed environment and, chiefly because it had been able to formulate and embody goals corresponding to important social problems, had achieved a very strong position on the market. But as the social problems lost some of their urgency the environment became freer. At the time of our study, the company's 50% share of the market had shrunk to a mere 20%. Despite these problems and the consequent drop in profitability, the company felt unable on moral grounds to transfer their resources to certain expanding submarkets where profit could easily be made. To exploit such 'luxury' markets was 'immoral': a cooperative firm should try to create 'healthy' consumer habits.

> When an organization is accused of having become a 'state within the state', it often turns out to be an appendix organization which has become an institution but which is still expected by its principal to maintain a subordinate position. The Transport Administration Office was involved in a conflict of this kind in 1966–1967. The minister responsible appointed a commission to investigate the organization of the Office and another to formulate its long-term goals. But the Office had already gone too far towards becoming an institution, so that any attempt at reincorporating it as an appendix organization was bound to fail. Both the commissions had to depend mainly on the Office's own experts, and in the case of the organizational investigation the Office had to take over the major part of the work.

Consonance through Dominance

We have seen that certain types of organization tend towards a relatively trouble-free existence in certain types of environment. There is, however, no guarantee of this. Many corporations and marginal organizations get into difficulties even in a free environment; we can also find maladjusted appendix organizations in a political environment and institutions with problems in a mixed one.

Nevertheless, the above classification is not without significance; the processes employed by the different types of organization in solving their adaptation problems are, after all, essentially different.

We can examine below some of the ways in which a corporation can become consonant with its environment. First, however, we must eliminate a common misconception, namely that the corporation can gain some sort of advantage in predicting environmental change.

On the Predictability of Environmental Change

The environment of an organization is a system of interdependent components. Interdependencies reveal themselves, for example in the exchange of goods and information; they are also closely bound up with various kinds of irreversible change. Changes on one market link up with changes on others; they also depend on changes in the age and educational structure of the population and, consequently, on the labour market; they are affected by general economic trends and are therefore dependent on the supply of capital, etc. During the period 1955–1965 the environment of the partly state-owned Development Company changed in a number of ways.

In 1955 commercial nuclear energy was a futuristic dream of uncertain destiny; by 1965 most power plants built were nuclear energy stations. In 1955 enriched uranium was available only in the USA and England; by 1965 it was a commercial raw material, subject to state controls but in principle available to nuclear power plants in practically all countries. In 1955 Swedish industry's interest in questions of atomic energy was polite but hazy; no practical steps were taken. In 1965 the General Industrial Company was fighting to survive as an electrotechnical company and regarded nuclear energy as one of its main products. In 1955 there was an acute shortage of university-trained engineers; in 1965 there were plenty of engineers—in fact underemployment threatened. In 1955 every political party had its active minority which claimed that Sweden should develop and manufacture atomic weapons. By 1965 Sweden had signed an international agreement against the spread of nuclear weapons, thus eliminating any such possibility. In 1955 a nuclear power station was thought to be a serious threat to society. By 1965 many people had come to believe that nuclear energy provided a golden opportunity for avoiding air pollution and saving large areas of natural mountain scenery from the disfiguring effects of hydroelectric power.

In any attempt to project the future, it is important to be able to treat the environment as a system. Various forecasting methods have therefore been developed with this very purpose: to map the environment as a system. Input–output and growth models have been developed in most countries and these have provided a basis for long-range plans. Similar attempts have been made on a restricted scale to design models of different industries. Growth models can also be used for simulating alternative courses of development. Games have been developed for similar purposes, particularly in military circles, e.g. to simulate possible future strategic states. Qualitative forecasts of the environment, which have been dubbed scenarios, describe alternative future states, and seeing the environment as a system they synchronize the different elements in this description of the future environment.

All these forecasting methods are now being tried out by various companies as part of their long-range planning. In our material we came across attempts to work out qualitative scenarios of Sweden's public administration 1975 (long-range plan, Registration Office) and quantitative system models of the house-building trade. Most experiences have been noticeably negative, something which may of course depend on weaknesses in the models used. But before we accepted this explanation, we wanted to look again at some of the assumptions that generally lie behind environmental forecasts.

Any reasonably reliable forecast will be based on the assumption that the forecaster commands a complete model of the system concerned, and that the model is closed. In other words the forecaster knows or can control the future states of all the variables that will influence the system from outside (exogenous variables). Forecasts of economic developments, for example, are extremely uncertain since the economy of any one country will always depend on economic developments in other countries. Thus, some assumptions will always have to be made about international economic developments, and the forecast will only be successful in so far as these assumptions prove correct. In making market models, the model builder usually 'closes' his model by assuming certain general economic developments, or assuming that there will be no change in taste or fashion. By making this second assumption he is ignoring the market's dependence on various social conditions outside the model.

Free actors in a system (e.g. the members of an organization, or the companies in an economy) represent a further source of unpredictability. Models containing such components are 'open' unless it can be assumed that the forecaster knows the goals and values of the actors and can predict any possible changes. Market models, for example, often ignore this fact, again perhaps by assuming that tastes will remain unchanged. We will later show how unrealistic such assumptions often turn out to be.

However, the inherent unpredictability of an open model can be eliminated without resort to such unrealistic assumptions: the forecaster can take control of developments, thereby compensating for the interference that can otherwise be caused by the unpredictable environment. Here, however, we must bring in the laws of dominance referred to earlier, for example Ashby's law of requisite variety. According to this, uncertainty can only be completely removed if the person controlling the system commands a countermeasure for every disturbance that might be generated by the environment. If the controller has to create or manufacture countermeasures in advance he must of course also be able to predict possible alternative developments in the environment.

If a system is controlled by some other person and he commands a requisite variety of countermeasures, then knowledge of the controller's goals will increase the predictability of future developments in the system. An economy controlled by a strong government commanding a rich variety of economic-political tools will be much more predictable than a less controlled economy. Honeywell seems to have recognized this fact and has designed a model accordingly. On this basis the company hopes to be able to predict which fields of research will be assigned most importance by the federal government at different times in the future. The company has assumed the existence of three federal goals (non-combat, military and exploration) which guide government action. Repeated forecasting success has been claimed for this model. It seems unlikely, however, that certain recent developments—e.g. increasing research into particular social problems—will have been foreseen.

Thus, we have identified three main situations affecting the reliability of predictions of the future state of a system:

1. If the forecaster commands a closed system model that is as complex (or complete) as the real situation it describes, he can predict the development of the system.

2. The above condition is not necessary provided that the forecaster can command countermeasures and can control the system. Only a requisite variety of countermeasures is then necessary; this means that the forecaster must have some idea of the type of disturbances likely to arise in the environment.

3. If the model is incomplete, or the forecaster lacks a requisite variety of countermeasures (control tools), he cannot predict the development of the system. Presumably, too, the more incomplete the model and the greater the gap between expected disturbances from outside and his powers of control, the less likelihood there is of his predictions being realized.

Experience shows that for an organization to predict environmental developments in their entirety would be a task of unreasonable proportions. Nor would there be any point in making the effort, since it would never be possible to use the information. The problem must be limited: perhaps the organization tries to predict a part of the environment close to it, or some other part that is of particular interest.

Whether or not it is possible to regard the immediate environment as closed depends chiefly on where its boundaries are drawn. An example is provided by recent attempts to forecast the location of industry, where the authorities concerned failed to control a subsystem because it was too dependent on other subsystems. Admittedly the 'forecaster' had a complete model (a map showing the location of industry), but the control tools available were not adequate (they lacked the requisite variety) to counter-act the powerful forces of the larger system (the whole economy).

Land development by building companies provides another example from our material. A land-owning building firm can easily make a plan or model of its development projects. But since these firms are dependent on other subsystems (municipal authorities, competitors, general economic policy as it affects the demand for housing, etc.) there is no guarantee that they can predict the outcome of their plans. As a result, builders generally have to approach things differently. In Sweden they often submit to a municipal plan. The local authority on the other hand generally has pretty tight control over the housing market, achieved by depriving the private consumer of his freedom of choice.

Sometimes, however, we find companies failing although they appeared to command comprehensive environmental models and a requisite variety of control tools. One of the best known examples is provided by Ford. The company hoped to gain control of a part of the medium-price automo-bile market by introducing the Ford Edsel. The attempt failed: a basic change in taste hit the market; it had not been foreseen and no counter-measures were available.

Thus, under certain conditions organizations can predict developments in the immediate environment. The immediate environment must consist of a subsystem which is more or less closed; the forecaster must have knowledge of the disturbances generated by the secondary environment and likely to affect the system he seeks to control; the forecaster must command a requisite variety of countermeasures. If these conditions are not fulfilled, it is not possible to predict developments even in the immediate environ-ment. Environmental studies and incomplete models may of course be of great value in other contexts.

The Corporation Needs to Dominate Its Environment

Thus, developments in the environment can be forecast only by the person or persons dominating the environment and, consequently, governing its development. This is important for organizations with internal goals: *corporations (and, as we shall see later, institutions) must dominate their environment if they are to be able to fulfil their own internal (strategic) planning.* Only thus can the corporation compensate for the inevitable uncertainty of all environmental forecasting.

> One of the companies we studied illustrates an interesting case: considerable uncertainty in forecasting the environment was transformed into almost complete certainty in a long-range plan. The conquest of a new geographical market previously dominated by several small companies had been set up as a major strategic goal. The future was extremely uncertain. One competitor at least was likely to go bankrupt. A merger between two of the others was a possibility. There was also a feeling that one or two of them might be open to purchase. Starting from a 'decision tree' the management of 'our' company could lay claim to a counter-measure for every possible course of development, such that their desired goal was assured. Uncertainty at the forecasting stage had been transformed into complete certainty in planning. Barely two years later the company achieved its goal.

An organization that cannot thus dominate its environment, but which behaves as though it could predict environmental developments and designs long-range operational plans accordingly, is almost sure to run into serious difficulties. The Forestry Company provides an interesting example. At an earlier stage in its life the company had been able to dominate its environment; it was used to making meaningful long-range plans. In time, however, lower overseas transport costs opened the European market—previously dominated by the company—to all kinds of disturbances from non-European markets. The situation had changed radically.

> In the mid-1950's the Swedish government decided to exert its right, invested in a long-standing agreement, to buy from the Forestry Company large forest resources in the north of Sweden. Thus the company suddenly found itself with almost half a billion crowns available for new investment. During the next three years most of the necessary investment policy was decided upon. Some of the resources were used for various measures to improve efficiency and some for the expansion of an area of forest land. About a hundred million crowns were invested in renewing the company's transport system. But the largest share was invested in a big manufacturing plant for the production of, mainly, Kraft paper. It was felt that this would answer the raw material requirements of certain industries. Unfortunately, the investment coincided with an economic downswing and a considerable over-production of Kraft paper. Changes in pulp prices and transport

costs only made things worse. It turned out afterwards that hardly any of the forecasts or profitability estimates on which the company had based its many large investments had been correct in any respect.

Some Ways of Achieving Dominance

As we can see from the general discussion in Chapter 2 and from the examples quoted above, there are various ways in which dominance can be achieved. The company which could transform an uncertain forecast into a certain plan fulfilled Ashby's requirement: it dominated because it commanded a requisite variety of countermeasures. One of the commonest examples of this way of achieving dominance is the company that can control developments in its sales volume, for instance by manipulating its prices or varying its geographical market. Volvo, for example, enjoys unusual opportunities for dominating its environment, including long-term developments and, therefore, for governing developments in sales. On many of its markets the company does not use all the means of competition available to achieve maximum sales; it can also vary the rate at which new markets are established. Thus two tools are immediately available for counteracting any disturbance on the market. Few companies are in as favourable a position as Volvo when it comes to planning investments, production, personnel resources, etc.

In the long-range plan designed for Karl Westlund & Co. an attempt was made to achieve a similar position. Here too there were opportunities, as yet unused, of establishing operations on other geographical markets. But to be able to dominate the environment and plan company developments, it is also necessary in such a situation to increase capital reserves (establishment often requires big investments) and, even more importantly, to build up personnel reserves.

A monopolist can often make use of a rather similar mechanism to counteract disturbances from the environment, namely by varying the satisfaction of consumer needs.

Our chief example of a monopolist in a position to dominate its environment was the General Hospital. Here the opportunities for long-range planning were almost ideal. There were of course some uncertain factors regarding population development in the local county council area, but since it was anyway impossible to satisfy all possible medical needs, the planning problem could simply be reformulated: how could the economic resources

available best be utilized? To some extent technological developments could also be ignored, since medical developments would
obviously advance more rapidly than the necessary economic and
personnel resources could be made available.

On a competitive market the organization that wishes to dominate will
have to enjoy some sort of superiority. But since we have assumed that
the organization and its environment are both complex systems, and that
in such systems changes in single components rarely lead to any significant
change in the functioning of the system as a whole, *it will be difficult to
achieve dominance through the improvement of single components. To
gain any significant advantage it will generally be necessary to change the
whole system.*

The frozen food industry provides a classic example. Before the pro-
moters of frozen food could achieve a position of domination many radical
changes were necessary. Distributors and consumers had to acquire the
necessary freezers; consumers had to learn how to use the new products;
raw material suppliers had to adapt their products and production to the
new method. Two other industries—computers and defence—have consciously defined their production as a system. From them we have learned
that if a system is to dominate its environment, the 'hard' components
(material products) are not the only factor that counts. Often the different
types of service offered, and other 'soft' components, are equally important.

The tourist industry, the toy industry, the entertainment industry, the
oil companies, the packaging industry and soon large parts of the public
sector such as telephones, power, and medical care, will have managed
successfully to consolidate their position by thinking in system terms. The
power industry provides a large-scale example of an attempt to develop
and introduce into the environment a new and superior system solution.
The industry has encouraged consumers to transfer on a grand scale to
electric house heating, using a combination of traditional power stations
and plants of entirely new types, e.g. nuclear power and pump power
stations. This method of dominating the environment is so important to
the corporation—although used with varying success in different
industries—that I will devote a special section to its study.

Systems Development
A General Model. There are three important conditions which must be
fulfilled if an organization is (a) to develop systems and (b) to enforce their
acceptance on the environment.

First, the organization must design a systems blueprint. In simple cases
all that may be needed is an intuitive idea about the system, perhaps in
the mind of the business leader. In more complex cases there must be

detailed descriptions and a considerable amount of development work; often the simulation of alternative system formulations or other experiments.

Secondly, the organization must have resources available for search activities, in the environment or in some delimited part of it, so that opportunities for applying the system or any restrictions on its use can be discovered.

Thirdly, resources must be available for penetrating the environment which the system is intended to dominate. Here we include the resources needed for incorporating the system into the existing set-up (perhaps the production or distribution systems).

An Example. The story of Karl Westlund & Co. from its beginnings during the 1920's is an exciting one. New system descriptions are continually on trial; sometimes the area of search is extended; often limited resources narrowly restrict the possibilities. The founder describes the beginnings as follows:

> I was born into a farming family. Ours wasn't a big farm, just a medium-sized one. My father was a carpenter. He was an expert, just as I've become. I began as a builder's labourer. But first I should tell you that as far as I know there were no trained builders in that part of northern Sweden at that time. Anyone with a bit of know-how and push took on building jobs under contract. In time I became one of them. Three of us were in it together. We worked very hard and began to earn quite a bit. In time we began to do jobs for the various local authorities in those parts. They provided the materials themselves. That suited us as we hadn't got much behind us. We got several schools and homes through them. This was at the beginning of the 20's, about 1924–25. Towards the end of the 20's we began to provide our own materials and things were going very well. We earned a lot of money; we'd tasted blood.

At the beginning of the 1930's however, came the depression; Westlund lost all his savings. But he continued to extend his area of search and began to make a bid for larger buildings, schools, etc. He goes on:

> Competition was so harsh in our parts that we felt it was time to move on. At home we couldn't keep afloat: 13 or 14 bids for every job. There were lots of small builders who'd come up the same way I had, they were going bankrupt one after the other. If you're too small, you have to pack it in.

So we moved to a larger town up there, and it was pretty tough.
We were up against some hard types. There wasn't much for us at
first, but we managed to keep going. Gradually things got better.
We got a few jobs in a neighbouring town, but it wasn't too good
there. I don't know how much we lost. I never found out. We built
bakeries and slaughterhouses in the first town we'd moved to,
along the railroad. We'd quite a lot on the go there.

Thus Westlund's first attempt to find an environment to dominate was
based on the system 'skilled labour—hard work—own forest', while an
important feature of the attempt to establish operations in the larger towns
was the supply of trained building engineers: his own son with two
colleagues. The son took on a buying manager, built up a budget system
and took various steps to rationalize operations. He also nursed a vision
of a system on a grander scale altogether. He and his contemporaries had
dreams of moving south and building small homes. Other system ideas were
also discussed; some were even tried out. One was to develop the firm
into an all-round building company with its own construction department;
another was to join a Swedish consortium for building homes in Africa.
The only change that achieved any success was on a smaller scale: it
involved another move and a changeover to larger projects. An attempted
changeover to a completely new production method, at the same time
establishing the firm on the Stockholm market, nearly ended in bankruptcy.
And at the time of our investigation the company was battling with a
new half-finished system idea involving factory-built small homes. It is
interesting to read the president's summary of the basic ideas behind this
vision.

Since 1957 we had been building small homes in quite large
groups. This was really a development of our traditional line;
production followed the pattern to be found in other types of
house-building. Many features were irrational; costs were considerable. Cost-wise results were not what, purely theoretically, we
would have expected. A big weakness was that our constructions
covered a wide ground area and the natural building material,
which up here is wood, gave rise to a lot of refund claims since
wood is a living material. The quality was not what it should be
for the best results. The building of family homes was often
interrupted during the winter. Apartment houses are built up-
wards on a fairly small ground area. Then winter matters less.
We struggled with it, but couldn't cope with any really big
changes.

Since 1963 we've been very busy with the administrative side of things, reconstructing the company economically. We'd had a liquidity crisis and various other reforms had to be dealt with. When we'd cleared that up we began to think about other things, for instance the home-building side. It had become increasingly clear over the years that there was no future in loose timber building as a production method. Also there were fewer labourers around with experience of timber building; it was difficult to recruit men to do a good-quality job and, since they were not used to the work, they didn't do too well on piece rates. This made it more difficult than ever to get good men and we were under great pressure to make some sort of change. And anyway we wanted to be on the band-wagon. But mainly we were driven by a desire to solve our problems on the small-homes side, because this was something that we had a very strong feeling for. Particularly since we felt there was room there for new business. As a sector it was less subject than others to controls and political influence.

Control and Homogenization. Domination of the environment, as the phrase is used in this report, should not be confused with other concepts such as market share. Since we use 'dominate' in the sense of 'ability to control changes', it is quite possible that a company that does not command the largest share of the market in a particular industry may nevertheless dominate, i.e. be able to control developments, although this is perhaps not very usual. On the car market in the USA, for example, Chrysler or Ford seem at various times to have been the leading figures, i.e. they could devise new ideas, 'concepts' and compel their acceptance. In so far as competitors do not react quickly enough and the smaller company has sufficient resources to follow up any such success, it is of course probable that the dominating company will also come to enjoy the largest market share.

The Interior Decorating Company's market share reflects the company's position fairly well. A few decades ago the company was a marginal and not particularly successful organization. It then managed to devise a completely new product and a completely new production set-up, thus creating a market for a type of consumer capital goods which had not previously existed. As we have described elsewhere this dominating position has gradually disappeared as competitors have copied the idea. Today the company does not dominate its environment nor does it command the largest market share.

The main task of marketing, and particularly of advertising, is to homogenize the part of the environment—e.g. the market segment—that the corporation has chosen. Only thus can it achieve the complete consonance required between its own (production) system and the environment's (consumption) system.

I once discussed with some American students the ways in which different types of organization adapt to changes in the environment. The following day one of the students told me of a dream he had had. It was about a corporation's need to homogenize its market.

> It was like a balloon, or perhaps an airship, moving over the landscape. It had a long thick tail dragging along the ground and a nose like a blow-pipe. Soon I noticed on its tail the words Popcorn Corporation and as it came past me it blew a spray of popcorn into my mouth. Nice, warm popcorn. My first fear disappeared. Now I understood how the ship worked. Through its tail it gathered up corn from the ground and now I could see that the whole ship was made of corn cobs. And all the time the ship grew and grew, spitting out more and more popcorn. And its tail flattened the earth. What had been rather uneven ground with some forest land became great, flat fields of corn. And then I saw a kind of spaceman figure; he stepped out and began to organize the people on the ground who were gaping, all the time eating popcorn. Some of the people didn't want to sit still and when one of the creatures came up to me—he had PCC on his shirt—I too felt rather restless. But then a TV appeared in front of me and I calmed down. And it felt just fine.

Consonance through Mapping

Naturally, an organization which can develop superior systems, and which can use these to dominate its environment, is in an advantageous position, not least because it can formulate internal goals and make plans for their fulfilment. But by no means all organizations enjoy such a position, a fact which is not acknowledged in the literature. Many organizations lack internal goals, but not because of neglect on the part of management. Often, on the contrary, the lack of goals represents a necessary adjustment to circumstances. Our study taught us dearly that it is very difficult for the non-dominating organization to operate the type of long-range planning employed by the corporation.

> To start with, in both the Interior Decorating Company and the Provincial Savings Bank, we tried with some success to interest management in some sort of long-range planning. But the attempts

soon had to be abandoned, mainly because in any prediction of the environment we—management and consultants—were overwhelmed by the number of uncertain factors. From this point on, however, the two organizations chose rather different paths. At the Interior Decorating Company management sounded out the possibility of developing some new system idea which would reinstate the company in its previous dominating position. The Bank, on the other hand, sought the best way of continuing operations without reliance on a long-range plan.

The organization which cannot forecast enviromental change will have to find some other way of becoming consonant with its environment. The main hypothesis to emerge from our case studies was that the successful marginal organization achieves consonance through mapping. I have described this mechanism in Chapter 4 and suggested four main conditions for its success. These can now be slightly reformulated to suit our present context, as follows:

1. As a result of external environmental change or internal dissatisfaction, the organization must be exposed to new environmental elements with new demands.
2. The organization must possess the resources necessary for finding new answers to the demands of the environment.
3. The organization must have an adequate information system and some sort of yardstick for evaluating the success of these answers.
4. The organization must have some mechanism for confirming and maintaining the successful answers or mappings of the environment.

Our proposition—that marginal organizations achieve consonance through mapping—is reminiscent of another suggestion sometimes made in the literature (e.g. March and Simon, 1958, and Cyert and March, 1963), namely that organizations can learn. However, this has never been developed properly into a theory. The writers concerned have simply intimated that analogies with psychological learning theories might be fruitful. From the two main schools of learning theory—stimulus-response theory (e.g. Skinner) and the various cognitive theories (e.g. Tolman)—we can derive two quite different explanations of the type of organizational change usually described as organizational learning. Simon and his followers have described organizational learning as an extension or change of programme; they claim that if a change in programme is rewarded, it will be made permanent. This explanation appears to owe most to Skinner's theory of learning. For instance, there is no assumption that anyone in the organization is aware of the learning process; at any rate it is not postulated that any central body, such as management or a development department, perceives the change and makes a conscious decision about it. On the other hand, it does not seem unreasonable to suppose that the more or less conscious perception of a change and the related planning and decision making, constitutes an important phase in the learning process. Some of our cases tend to confirm that some kind of stimulus-response model often best explains the first phase in the adaptation process of the marginal organization, but that at a later stage organizations usually make a more conscious effort to legitimatize and formalize an established adjustment, partly at least in the cause of internal efficiency.

New Environmental Experiences and New Solutions to the Demands of the Environment

Organizations differ greatly in the opportunities available to them for meeting new environments and trying to satisfy new demands. Some highly specialized organizations in closed environments with few stakeholders practically never come into contact with new environments at all. Organizational structure can also affect the issue: for instance a company without any sales or marketing organization of its own will find itself cut off from many nourishing environmental contacts. For this reason Burns and Stalker (1961) go so far as to warn companies against the specialization and centralization of environmental contacts. Burns has described two types of organization structure, the mechanistic and the organic, and postulated that in a rapidly changing environment the organic or little formalized structure is superior to the mechanistic or highly formalized. We did not find that this always agreed with our experience: there seemed to us to be some most successful mechanistic organizations in unstable environments. On the other hand, in the case of the marginal organization, the accuracy of Burns' description was confirmed. According to Burns the organization can achieve the ability to discover new solutions to environmental problems by avoiding mechanistic structures and layers of 'translators' to interpret the demands of the environment at different levels. This picture seems to match pretty well our idea of the way the successful marginal organization works. But the situation of the large organization which can develop systems and dominate its environment is quite different. A mechanistic structure of the type described by Burns is then often of vital importance. It provides the best framework for a disciplined development of systems and for the demanding task of getting a major system accepted by the environment.

I would like to add something to Burns' description of the organic organization structure: it seems to me that various policies and values can encourage, or of course discourage, the acquisition of new environmental experiences and the discovery of new solutions to environmental problems. 'We are a food industry.' 'We must devote ourselves primarily to the most difficult projects of the large customer.' 'As far as possible we must engage ourselves in international cooperation.' 'The young are our future customers—we must learn to recognize their tastes and needs.' Organizations often appear to rejoice in such creeds; they serve to rivet attention, and provide a light by which to interpret new experiences. Obviously, though, rules like this—which themselves can be seen as the result of learning processes—may be destructive if they cut the organization off from new environments where it might have greater opportunities for development. Levitt has discussed this.

> The railroads did not stop growing because the need for passenger and freight transportation declined. That grew. The railroads are in trouble today not because the need was filled by others (cars, trucks, airplanes, even telephones), but because it was *not* filled by the railroads themselves. They let others take customers away from them because they assumed themselves to be in the railroad business rather than in the transportation business. The reason they defined their industry wrong was because they were railroad-oriented instead of transportation-oriented; they were product-oriented instead of customer-oriented. (Levitt, 1960, p. 45)

Evaluation of New Environmental Experiences and Maintenance of Successful Mappings of the Environment
One of the greatest advantages enjoyed by the traditional business company with a simple profit goal and a satisfactory system of internal accounting is that it can easily judge the success of new operations, new products or other experiments. If in addition the company possesses a decentralized structure, making possible the retention of profits, it has at its disposal a built-in mechanism for maintaining successful mappings of the environment.

If agencies of public administration are judged according to such a pattern, they will often have to be pronounced extremely unsuccessful. Since their goals are manifold and sometimes conflicting, there can rarely be any unambiguous criterion of success. There will often be a time-lag before the central agency, which allocates resources, discovers the success and confirms its continuation. The Registration Office and the General Hospital provided many examples of ambitious experiments, all aimed at improving the organization's ability to satisfy environmental demands, which were never evaluated by those with resources at their command, let alone supported and promoted as prototypes in other parts of the organization. On the contrary, organizations of this type seem to contain mechanisms that pull hard in the opposite direction. Certain units of the Development Company that had been successful in satisfying special environmental demands were thought of as 'awkward', particularly as they kept on asking for more resources. (That these units generated at least as much in the way of resources as they asked for was rarely mentioned in the government accounts.)

Sometimes, though, we noticed that the ordinary business company could also be surprisingly ineffective in its learning activities.

> The Construction and Building Company and the Forestry Company tended particularly to engage in explorative experimental operations, probing completely new environments. They might, for example, acquire a subsidiary in a new line of business or experiment with totally new types of products. So far so good. But these experiments were not evaluated in any way that reflected their nature. The companies in fact acquired much useful knowledge that could have provided a basis for the development of systems with subsequent domination of a market. Nevertheless, these operations were judged on the same grounds as the other well-established lines of business i.e. for their economic result. And on these grounds, of course, they were often a 'failure'. Thus we found numerous experiments with new markets, abandoned after a time with something learned—and with certain losses made.

Another common fault, not to be confused with the above, is an inability to learn from past failures: not to reduce unprofitable operations, not to withdraw when the market is no longer willing to reward the company for its contributions. According to af Trolle (1967), this is one of the commonest causes of economic difficulties. A study of the operations of some Swedish publishers seemed to show that just this ability, to learn from misfortune, made all the difference between the successful marginal organization and the others.

> One publisher actually suggested that the ability to 'jump on the bandwagon' was necessary for success in the trade. Another one had had an opportunity to show his ability in this kind of learning: when he saw that his business was no longer running profitably in its present form, he cut down his sales corps by 80% at very short notice. A third had already decided to withdraw from the book business, although not entirely: he was holding on to some resources and keeping an eye on developments; in the meantime he transferred his remaining resources to another trade.

Consonance through Matching

Like the marginal organization the appendix organization has to adapt to its environment although it is unable to dominate, or govern, developments.

On top of this, the appendix organization also has to make its external goals agree with those of the environment. This involves the process of adaptation that I have called matching (see Chapter 4). Thus I postulate that the appendix organization must somehow be able to identify and and understand the problems and the strengths of its principal and aim to match them. Of all the problems of adaptation that we met, those of the appendix organization were generally among the most difficult. Other types of organization can do much to guide their own development; the appendix organization has to depend entirely on its principal. The tendency of appendix organizations towards institutionalization or stabilization reflects an attempt to free themselves from this restrictive situation. Very little has been written about the adaptation problems of appendix organizations. Wodehouse (1934) appears to be one of those who has some insight into the difficulties.

> Jeeves, the perfect manservant, is utterly loyal to his master until Lord Bertie Wooster formulates an internal goal incompatible with Jeeves' own: Bertie is going to learn the banjulele. When Lord Bertie refuses to abandon this internal goal, one solution remains: Jeeves hands in his notice and attaches himself as an appendix organization to another master. But as various complications ensue, Jeeves is frequently called to Lord Bertie's aid. Bertie's need for 'matching' is painfully clear. In the end it becomes so strong that the banjulele disappears and Jeeves returns to his former positon. (Wodehouse, 1934)

Unhappily not every appendix organization enjoys such freedom of choice and it is not so easy to abandon a parent organization that has formulated incompatible goals.

Parent Organizations with Internal Goals
Before studying the more complex problems of the appendix organization, we must look at a class of comparatively simple situations. Suppose that the parent organization (government department, parent company, other organization) dominates its environment and is thus able to set up long-term internal goals; the external goals of the appendix organization will probably develop out of this internal planning. The total system that can be designed by the planner or planners in the parent organization covers the organization and the environment, including the appendix unit. The General Hospital provides a typical example.

> The County Council's long-range plan for medical care was based on various forecasts covering market and technological

developments. Population forecasts and other statistics provided a basis for assessing future medical care requirements; facts and figures gleaned from a variety of public investigations formed grounds for an estimate of the special techniques and other technological innovations that could be expected during the coming 10-year period. Since the organization dominated its environment as a monopoly, it could easily translate the forecasts into plans for building, training, recruitment and financing. In these plans the General Hospital was assigned a specific role. It would be expected increasingly to undertake certain coordinating tasks; at the same time it would be relieved of a certain amount of out-patients work. There were of course a few uncertain points and others that were not as clear as could have been desired. But on the whole the plans clarified the external goals of the organization with an explicitness that was rare in the organizations we studied. And, moreover, this was in an environment of very rapid technological change.

Parent Organizations without Internal Goals

Most appendix organizations, however, view their situation differently. During our investigations we were almost always told by the appendix organizations that the parent unit was quite incapable of formulating goals: perhaps the principal was a government department with more important problems on hand, or a parent company that did not recognize or did not want to admit the difficulties it was causing its subsidiary by unclear or irrelevant goals. Sometimes, like the partly state-owned Development Company, an appendix organization eventually asks its principal to appoint a commission to formulate new goals; in other cases a strategic management group emerges in the appendix organization, taking control of future developments and stabilizing and institutionalizing the organization. Such a development may cause new problems at a later stage, with conflicts between the self-appointed leaders and the parent organization whose interest in its subsidiary may have been reawakened.

The above discussion has already suggested my view of this type of problem. Usually the problems are inevitable; the principal does not dominate the environment and cannot therefore formulate internal goals for itself or external goals for its subsidiary or appendix organization. It is wrong to blame the difficulties on the principal. The appendix organization cannot simply demand a goal. Unfortunately, in our discussions with appendix organizations, we often made this mistake ourselves. The possibility of other solutions must be investigated.

The Dominating Appendix Organization

Should the management of an appendix organization accept the external goals prescribed by the principal? This question faced the Transport Administration Office.

> TAO's job is to make investments and oversee the running of a major part of the public sector. Developments in technology have continually increased the importance of this task and during one 10-year period investments rose from 150 million to almost 2,000 million crowns. We could say that the traditional goal of the organization has been to allocate investments as 'fairly' as possible among different geographical areas and, within each area and together with representatives for local interests, to plan the details of the investments in a manner best suited to the problems of the region. Various environmental changes have rendered this goal increasingly irrelevant: population growth is being increasingly concentrated to three large conurbations while the rest of the country suffers varying degrees of depopulation; some regions are in difficulties due to structural changes in the local industry; international cooperation has become an increasingly important factor. The director general of TAO claimed that the minister responsible was completely in the power of 'parochial' politicians and was quite unable to formulate external goals better suited to the present situation. He thus concluded that TAO should formulate new external goals on its own, despite the conflict with the ministry that this would entail.

When the case is described in these terms, there seems little doubt about what should be done. We did not hesitate: our task, as we saw it, was to help the director general, among other things, to acquire resources sufficient for the formulation of goals and the subsequent embodiment of goals in the organizational structure. In its extreme form such a solution implies that the appendix organization tries to dominate its parent. In this case, however, TAO still accepted the common external goals—the relevant national policy—as the basis for its own planning. But, in another case, the appendix organization might come to regard its principal as a part of the exploitable environment. Imagine, for example, a state research laboratory such as Honeywell making a model of the decision-making authorities in Washington and using it as a basis for planning (Larsen, 1965). If the principal can be persuaded to use such a decision model, consonance has been achieved not by matching but by domination. This is more or less what we suggested at the Computer Centre, although we never consciously formulated such a policy to ourselves.

The Computer Centre is a data-processing unit, owned by a group of cooperative insurance companies in Sweden. In May 1964 we were called in to advise the company on its long-range planning and development work. In particular the Centre wanted to develop administrative control systems to sell to the owners (the customers). It was felt that the insurance companies needed help not only with their 'production' but with their internal planning and control as well. After making a preliminary analysis we realized that the organizational structure, range of products, and production methods of the insurance industry, would be changing radically in the next ten years or so and that any system of control, geared to the solving of present problems, would be out-of-date before it could even be made ready for use.

Together with the director general of the Computer Centre we tried to persuade some of the main customers to tell us about their long-term plans; we soon realized that they did not have any. In fact, the people with whom we came in contact showed no sign of wanting or being able to design such plans. We therefore decided together with the Centre to design a general model of the industry and, using this as our starting-point, to make a plan or forecast of developments in the cooperative insurance companies. We soon realized that many of the changes in which the companies were apparently involved represented no more than an attempt to imitate the large private insurance firms rather than to find an independent path. It seemed to us that our original analysis of the companies' distinctive competence could provide a basis for an alternative long-range plan. We sketched out such a plan and showed the management of the Computer Centre how it would be able to control developments. We also presented our analysis to some of the insurance company heads. A fortnight later we were summoned before the director general and told that the Centre wanted to break the research contract as soon as possible. The director was satisfied with our reports but had been subjected to sharp criticism from members of his board: he had no right to initiate research into tasks outside the Centre's sphere of responsibility.

In retrospect I doubt the ethics of our approach in this case—a point to which I will return in Chapter 7. Here I simply want to show how an appendix organization can set about trying to dominate its principal.

The Dominated Appendix Organization

Let us now look at an example in which the principal clearly dominates its appendix organization but severe problems arise because the principal lacks internal planning. The situation as seen by the director general of the National Rationalization Office (NRO) can suffice as an example.

> NRO's task is to improve the efficiency of the public administra-
> tion. But this is not a sufficiently concrete goal to provide guide-
> lines for our activities. Our principal, the Minister of Finance,
> expects us to contribute to savings, particularly in personnel;
> that provides a possible concrete goal, supported by many
> members of our board. But a saving in personnel does not
> necessarily mean a saving in cost; both can be achieved in quite
> different ways. And anyway I'm not sure that this is the best goal
> for us. If we converted to EDP on a wide scale, we could probably
> cut down considerably the number employed in the public
> administration, but we'd probably only save very little in cost.
> Traditional work studies, organization studies of office work, help-
> ing to improve national budget and cost accounting systems—
> all these could lead to cost reductions. Finally, I feel that we must
> really strive to help the government agencies to utilize their
> resources more efficiently, for example by better personnel plan-
> ning, better management training, better information and decision
> systems, etc.

Thus, in the view of the director general, the problem was the existence of alternative goals of more or less equal importance; since resources were limited and the organization unable to cope with too great a variety of tasks, he felt forced to choose one of the possible concrete goals.

We did not make things easier for him by explaining, in the early days of our work together, that there was little point in trying to improve the efficiency of a complex system such as the public administration by attacking the problems of a limited area. New planning and information systems were no good unless department heads also received better training. Conversion to EDP would mean a review of the adjacent manual systems and so on. The only solution that our client could envisage was to divide the organization into smaller units, each of which would be able to attract new resources and fulfil its own particular task.

Gradually, however, an alternative emerged. NRO, and in particular the director general, learned to see the importance of matching the parent organization. Thus, the organization became deeply involved in building up resources, not only its own but also those of another closely related government agency, of the universities and commercial consultant firms and, most of all, of the agencies and authorities which it served. *In the course of this work NRO had to sacrifice certain possibilities for its own development. Leadership of an appendix organization often seems to demand this.*

Parent Organizations with Internal Conflicts
Sayles (1964) has shown that a leader's most important task is to protect his organizational unit from interference from above. Pelz and Andrews (1966) go further and claim that a successful leader must be able to represent his men effectively 'up the line'. The leader of an appendix organization is also expected to be able to do this, although it may of course restrict his readiness to sacrifice his own organization for the sake of matching the parent.

Granick (1954 and 1960) has provided some fascinating insights into the world's largest system of appendix organizations, i.e. industry in the USSR. This system, at least when Granick was studying it during the 1950's, could be said to consist of various units for the realization of plans and the achievement of goals prescribed by a central body. Granick's study shows very clearly that the successful leader must to some extent protect his unit from impossible demands from the 'parent organization'; often he must even break the law. The leader is faced with special problems whenever the parent organization is riven by internal conflict. I have chosen to reproduce one of Granick's examples, but I could easily have quoted several just as telling from our own material: the heads of government agencies, the subsidiaries of large industrial enterprises, and other appendix organizations studied by us, have often been in very similar situations.

> For over a year a Moscow director, S. A. Freiman, was threatened with legal action when he found himself in the middle of a quarrel between the Moscow City Council and his own Glavk. A house, formerly not under the plant, was transferred to the firm's ownership by an arbitrator of the Moscow City Council. Then the house was ordered repaired, and the firm's management was instructed to pay 40,000 rubels for this work. Director Freiman, however, would not pay, pleading that his Glavk refused to allocate him the necessary money as it denied that the house belonged to the firm, and that he could only get it by illegally taking it from funds specifically allocated to other purposes. The case dragged on, and finally director Freiman was sentenced by a Moscow court to six months of labour at his place of work with a 15% deduction from his pay. The court suspended sentence for four months, but the sentence was then to go into effect unless the repairs had meanwhile been completed. It is not recorded if the Glavk and the

Moscow City Council finally settled matters, or if Freiman actually had to decide which law he preferred to break. (Granick, 1954, p. 122)

Consonance through Joint Consultation

Institutions are up against a complex problem when it comes to achieving consonance between internal structure and environment. Like the corporation, the institution must reconcile its internal plans with a changing environment. This is only possible through dominance. However, the institution also resembles the appendix organization: it has to merge into a wider context. Difficulties can also arise because external and internal goals are not immediately compatible. I suggest that all three types of problem can be solved by the process described in Chapter 4 as *joint consultation*.

As we shall see, however, the problems of the institution are far from uniform. Let us look at two typical examples.

Institutions Adrift

An institution can in a sense be too successful: it may achieve its external goals and render its own continued existence unnecessary. In another case it can become superfluous because social developments make former goals irrelevant. The Provincial Savings Bank experienced a combination of these two situations.

The Provincial Savings Bank, like other similar banks, had based its success on three external goals: to promote saving, to offer security to savers, and to support the interests of the local community. For various reasons, however, it was now felt that these external goals required reassessment. Saving as a virtue had lost much of its former social importance; moreover, many other organizations now competed for any savings still made. The local community with which the Bank had originally identified itself, consisted now of two separate districts with essentially different problems: a depopulated area where even small one-man offices were becoming increasingly unprofitable, and another area that was economically—and would soon be politically—part of the neighbouring city. As the population grew, the total assets of the Savings Bank increased at a relatively faster rate than those of any other bank in the country. But this brought complications because the expansion required a similar increase in capital. At the same time profits were unsatisfactory, partly at least because of growing competition. Could the Bank really afford any goal other than profitability? Would it not be advisable to leave the depopulated area without bank offices, abandon the financing of home-building in the expanding area, and turn instead to whatever seemed to be the most profitable markets?

After the appointment of an administrative director and a new president, both coming from other organizations, a serious effort was made to formulate new goals more in keeping with the demands of the situation. When we studied the organization it exhibited an interesting example of conflicting goals. The financial director was concentrating on short-term credit to needy local authorities and, in general, to operations on the 'grey market'. The administrative director was planning the closure of non-profitable offices in the depopulated areas, and the development of a computer programme for sale as a complementary bank service to property-owners and small businessmen. The president, still trying to be a 'useful member of society', had found two main outlets for his activities: he helped customers to keep count of their vaccinations, innoculations, blood groups, etc., and encouraged the building of small low-cost homes.

The institution is adrift: it has lost touch with its former external goals and is searching urgently for new ones. What is important, what is to be its redefined mission? In such a situation, if it becomes serious, the company may show confusion and bewilderment in its behaviour. Here is another example.

Karl Westlund is 38 years old, but has been president ever since, as a man of 25, he took over the business from his father. He decided to abandon his university studies, but now that he has built up the company into one of the largest private industrial businesses in the far north of Sweden, with over 1,000 employees, he has no regrets. Our first job for him was to make a detailed study of the way the company had developed. We interviewed about 20 persons (inside and outside the company) who could be expected to throw some light on its values. Thus, we learned that Karl Westlund had been guided by one dominating goal: to provide development opportunities for able young people without private means. The composition of management, among other things, was proof of this. Most of its members had started as forestry or farm labourers; over a period of about ten years they had advanced to positions in top management. Someone told us, jokingly, that you had to be born north of the Arctic Circle to get anywhere in the company. The reasons for this situation were to be found chiefly in Karl Westlund's personal history. His father had started as a small farmer but had managed to provide eleven children with a decent education and a good start in life.

But the educational revolution had come to northern Sweden earlier than to any other part of the country. Difficulty in getting work provided one spur towards higher education: a larger proportion of the children here continued their schooling through junior college and even beyond. So the need to help young people was no longer as great as before. But this was not all. It was becoming increasingly clear that some relocation to areas of greater expansion was going to be necessary if the company was to be able to continue to develop. Even Karl Westlund admitted that some of his colleagues, albeit clever, were rather smug and unwilling to plan great exploits.

But what social problems and social goals was his organization best fitted to undertake? Ought he perhaps to engage himself in the employment problems of the locality? Or would that mean risking a company with good development possibilities for a task that might end in failure? Could he do anything about the problems of the developing countries? His right-hand man was sent to Africa to sound out the possibilities but came back with a negative report. Competiton was too harsh; the company lacked the right kind of resources. Could the company perhaps concentrate on products geared to the solution of important social problems such as air and water pollution? But again there were difficulties; research and development resources were insufficient for such a technical sphere. Karl Westlund began to show signs of an irresolution quite new to him. Suddenly he decided to resign as president; a few weeks later he withdrew his resignation. He announced that he and a few of his colleagues were going to move to the south of Sweden: this plan too was soon cancelled. He admitted that some sort of reorganization must be made, but put off doing anything about it.

Institutions with Incompatible External and Internal Goals
While the organization that has gone adrift has difficulty in finding external goals, other organizations are faced with almost the opposite problem. External goals can be a threat to survival if they are incompatible with internal ones. In some aspects the National Rationalization Office (NRO) illustrates this situation, but since the organization was not too highly institutionalized it could solve its dilemma by merging into a wider context,

more or less abandoning its internal goals. During our investigations we worked with three employers' and trade organizations, Alpha, Beta and Gamma, and there the problem was far more acute.

Membership of the three organizations overlapped; their tasks were also similar. They had all originated to support common interests and had developed increasingly into defence organizations. Their enemies were aggressive trade unions, financially strong suppliers, and a government that was very critical of the industry. We were called in because some of the members had expressed a long-felt need to merge, with a view to strengthening the joint organization and lowering the cost of membership. The president of Alpha took the final initiative; he acted as the driving force in a team consisting of three organization heads and two researchers.

It soon became obvious that the problem of goals was extremely complex. For a number of reasons a change in the industry was greatly to be desired on social grounds: the government and the trade unions were pressing for such a development, which would mean the end of many of the members as independent companies. An important feature of the situation was that, partly as a result of their hold on the wage structure of the industry the three organizations commanded a strong weapon in the battle for or against changes in the industry. But could a member organization work against the interests of the majority of its members? Similar problems arose because the short-term interests of some members seemed to be incompatible with those of society.

The attitude of the three heads towards these conflicting values seemed to vary from one occasion to the next. Perhaps they can be roughly summarized as follows.

It was unrealistic, according to the head of Gamma, to alter in any essential way the defensive character of the organizations. At the very first meeting the head of Beta asked: 'What am I? My members' representative or a servant of the interests of society?' The position was simplest for the head of Alpha: most of his members were leading companies which could expect to profit from changes in the industry. From the start he pressed for a merger of the three organizations; he called for active efforts to improve the efficiency of the industry and solve the problem of the small and inefficient members. On the last point he suggested that such members be offered adequate service so that the best of them could develop and adapt. The only point on which all the heads were agreed was: some sort of change must be made in external goals, or the organizations would gradually disintegrate, losing both status and power.

Some Examples

What do I mean by claiming that joint consultation offers a solution to the type of problem just described? Instead of answering my own question in general terms, I will comment on each of the three cases.

> The problem of the employers' organizations was a difficult one. Direct negotiations with the groups of members favouring retention of the defensive approach were hardly possible, at least in the initial stages. These groups were so dominating and powerful, particularly in Beta, that they could have gained almost any point they wanted. But, in so far as the leaders could free themselves from the domination of this group, a major task should have been to initiate joint consultation with the many bodies that a change in course would bring into the picture. Here, however, we came up against an interesting psychological problem. The defensive attitude had such deep roots that the idea of inviting the opponents (for instance a trade-union-run company) to discussions was simply not to be considered, at least not by the head of Gamma. The representatives of certain major social interests were also viewed with suspicion. The organizations feared that at any such consultations they would be betrayed, or forced to make too many concessions.

In a study of the US State Department, Argyris (1967) has claimed that an internal organization structure based on mistrust and on other values implicit in a traditional hierarchial structure, will project its suspicious attitude also into its external relations. The above case of the political organizations suggests that the opposite relation is more probable. If the external relations and goals of an organization encourage an attitude of conflict or defensiveness, the values and the techniques necessary to this aggressive external task will infect internal relations as well.

> A solution to the problems of NRO requires some attempt at stabilizing the expectations of the environment; this in turn means a willingness to discuss with representatives of other government agencies and similar organizations. Some sort of agreed picture must emerge of the future division of roles, in particular of the

role that NRO will be expected to play. This is roughly speaking the approach that has been chosen by the head of NRO; at the time of writing it is too early to judge the outcome.

Karl Westlund & Co. provides the clearest example of an organization which has chosen to solve its long-range planning by means of joint consultation. First Karl Westlund entered into joint consultation with representatives of the district in which his company had been operating. Could the company help to maintain employment in that part of the country? This matter was discussed and it was further questioned whether in fact it was reasonable for the company to take on such a task when it was also responsible for maintaining and developing its own resources. Thus, the company tried to identify with the problems and expectations of the local representatives and presented to them its own difficulties. In this way very fruitful discussions were born and a most generous offer was made by one of the authorities present. A large sum of public money was put at the disposal of the company for product development; it was hoped that results would benefit the local employment situation. In other discussions, too, fruitful common solutions were found; and the reputation of the company on the market and in the community where it operated is far higher than that enjoyed by any of the other organizations that we studied.

Supportive Systems and Defence Systems

Every writer who has studied structural change in organizations has noted that powerful stabilizing forces are present—forces that are important to short-term efficiency, but which can represent an obstacle to change. In Chapter 4 I described some of these forces as a defence system and noted particularly the importance of the political system. I will now describe some examples of this problem and try to characterize the political aspect in our four basic types of organization.

Marginal Organizations

The marginal organization has by definition neither external nor internal goals. Nevertheless, it sometimes manages to adapt to environmental change by means of a learning process, which makes very specific demands on its cognitive system. However, neither stimulating contact with the environment, nor a heightened ability to perceive and learn, will be of much value to the organization without a supportive system (particularly a power system) which makes possible the realization of the necessary changes, whether countermeasures or the exploitation of new opportunities.

In the very small company run by an owner-manager, one man is responsible for almost all contacts with the environment, and the situation is a straightforward one. The owner, the manager, the marketing director, the long-range planner—all in the same person—has unlimited power and right of decision.

In the somewhat larger marginal company, where more people are involved in external contacts, the matter is more complex. Here too, the cognitive system and the power system must coincide, i.e. all those responsible for identifying environmental changes and learning how to utilize or map the environments, must also be able to make decisions and have considerable freedom to make changes. Although the organization consists of several very independent units, the fact that it still is an organization, and the units enjoy common resources, means that there must be some sort of mechanism for weeding out inefficient activities. Otherwise the organization may find itself full of malignant tumours that eat up the resources introduced by their more healthy and successful neighbours.

The Construction and Building Company provides an example of a large marginal organization and the demands that face it. As in most building and construction firms, decentralization character- ized the organization of this company. Each local boss was in fact an independent entrepreneur, responsible for bidding, acquiring land and labour, internal training, supervision, etc. Between 1955 and 1960 the company consisted of roughly a dozen such units varying in size. The power plant unit worked in the far north, the road-building unit in the Stockholm region, the bridge- building unit was engaged on the construction of a big bridge; the recreation unit was aiming to exploit some large tracts of land, etc. At one time only the power plant unit was running profitably; the rest either ran at a loss, or at any rate made no profit. But management was not fully aware of this, or at least only realized the full impact of the situation when the losses were already a fact and the company had embarked on various new and in some ways equally unprofitable projects. This was partly because the com- pany had no system of internal budgeting or profitability analysis and, consequently, no quick way of getting reliable information about economic results, and partly because the president's position vis-à-vis the other bosses was not strong enough. Even if he ever felt that the company ought to suspend a particular branch of operations, central management was not in a position at that stage to carry out any quick decisions.

In this example I have, by implication, suggested the most common approach to the problem of weeding out inefficient units. Central management must be equipped with an information system by means of which each unit's result can be measured. The units may have almost unlimited freedom of action provided they are successful; but central management must have sufficient power and decisiveness to step in when results are unsatisfactory and either change the management of the unit concerned or close it down (sell it).

Appendix Organizations

The appendix organization has external goals which have been formulated by, or in consultation with, another organization (e.g. a government department or a parent company) or a small group (e.g. family owners) or a secondary group (an élite of some kind). It is most likely that this other organization or group retains control over the appendix organization and is one of its evaluators, possibly the main one. An important method of maintaining control is to appoint the leader of the appendix organization. The leader will be expected to pursue the prescribed external goals; consequently he will try in various ways to design an internal structure that supports them. However, this very link-up between external goals and a political structure will represent one of the most serious obstacles if for any reason a change becomes desirable.

> The Registration Office provides what is probably a fairly typical example of the problems of the political system in an appendix organization faced with changes in external goals. When a principal begins to make new demands on its appendix organization, this often reflects a shift in power within the principal's own set-up. To the appendix organization it is as though a new evaluator, making new demands, had arrived on the scene. In this case the Ministry of Finance was demanding with increasing insistence that all units in the public administration cooperate to improve efficiency and rationalize operations. The conflict between the Ministry's demand for rationalization and industry's demand for service was reflected in the Registration Office. Two parties emerged: one demanded loyalty to the principal, the other tried to oppose this, defending instead the original goal of high-quality service to industry.

There is no guarantee that the formal leader will also be the leader of the loyal party, particularly in an organization that is in the process of depoliticization or institutionalization. Such an organization is, *ipso facto*, trying to free itself from its principal and its leader is quite likely to be in the forefront of the opposition. This is probably why in so many countries new department heads are chosen not from inside the organization they are to lead but from the loyal ranks of the central government departments. This is what happened at the Registration Office. Soon after our work at the Office had been wound up, the director general retired and a new man was appointed from central government department (see Wallroth, 1968b).

We observed the same problem in a large industrial enterprise with numerous sales companies abroad. In general the heads of these subsidiaries did not support new external goals introduced by the parent organization; instead they showed passive and sometimes even active resistance. Again the only solution found was gradually to replace the dissenters by new men from the parent organization who identified with the change in goals. But other organizations have tried another solution: to bring about close and more intimate contact between appendix heads and parent organization. Several large companies have introduced comprehensive schemes for internal management training for just such a purpose. Other companies use yet another method: a rotation system. The head of a subsidiary must always be prepared for transfer to another country or back to the parent company. In family firms the traditonal solution is to make sure that all companies in the family's sphere of interest are run by members of the family.

Corporations

In Chapter 6 I will examine one of the major problems of the corporation: the problem of motivation. I will suggest there that the corporation formulates *quasi-goals* whose function is to 'glorify' the real internal goals. There are several other mechanisms for underpinning internal goals. Among the chief ones are: organization structure, reward system, planning system. However, these systems would have little meaning and less effect if they did not also represent a kind of promise on the part of management. The budget is not only a plan prescribed by management, it is also—and this is just as important—a promise made by management (cf. Cyert and March, 1963). So is the organization structure, so is the reward system: the implication is that provided an organizational unit fulfils its assigned role efficiently, it has the right to retain its position; if an employee satisfactorily meets the criteria for a raise, or a promotion, he has the right to receive them. It appears to be more usual for an employee to ask 'Why haven't I got the raise that I deserve?' than for management to say: 'Why don't you work harder so you can have a raise?'

In this way the organization structure and the reward system gradually define a structure, and a political system emerges to defend it. The research department will defend its research budget with all the means available; the engineers will defend their salary rights and promotion possibilities, etc.

Thus, the management of a corporation is walking a tightrope. A company may have resources for systems development, it may have formulated long-term internal goals; but of what use is this if, in its efforts to stimulate a high grade of performance, it has created a structure so strictly geared to the present situation as to preclude the possibility of change. How much power management will have to retain will depend basically on the nature of the necessary changes. If these involve an exchange of systems within the existing framework, the demands on the internal structure will be small. In the Forestry Company, for example, there was no difficulty in achieving a major change of great importance in the production systems of all divisions. But it proved impossible for years to make any decision about another change, involving a shift in equilibrium between certain branches of operations and requiring the creation of a completely new structure.

Institutions

The institution faces a problem that combines those of the appendix organization and the corporation. It must, like the corporation, design an internal structure that will motivate performance; like the appendix organization it has to deal with a principal and with members and others concerned mainly with external goals. As we have seen both these tasks have their attendant problems.

Beta experienced the labour conflict of 1932 as a critical event. The battle was lost chiefly because the member companies were not sufficiently united. It thus became important to design an organization structure to promote unity and to control the member companies, in order to serve the major external goal of fighting the enemy—the trade unions. A local association of employers was set up at every fairly large centre. The organization was generally speaking democratic. The power of the central organization was restricted, although in certain respects it remained considerable. Forty years later the external environment had altered radically; furthermore, growing internal resources had resulted in the development of a powerful administrative organization which was trying to establish internal goals. The Federation was faced with a difficult problem: to find new external goals just as internal goals were being designed and adapted to the old ones.

Management knew in the main what was wanted. Alpha and Beta should merge; close cooperation, if not a formal merger, should be established with Gamma. At the same time certain radical changes were needed to improve personnel resources. This was the internal goal.

The external goal was less clear. It was still essential to defend members against the trade unions but it was no longer the main task. More important was to structure the industry efficiently. In working for this goal the organization needed to regain the initiative from government and trade unions (the latter were directly involved as they owned a company in the industry).

These goals, both external and internal, emerged gradually in the course of a year. The heads of Alpha and Beta managed to cooperate with the somewhat hesitant head of Gamma and with the researchers. However, it gradually became obvious that it was not just a question of establishing goals: there were powerful obstacles to an adjustment, both internal and external, that would have to be overcome. The small members naturally wanted to maintain the status quo. What they needed was a defence organization; they showed little interest in a structural change in the industry. Naturally, the heads of the local organizations, and perhaps the rest of their staff, were also anxious to defend the present structure.

The choice of leader for the joint organization became the all-important political question. The three heads all had their supporters both in the administrative organization and in the member companies. In the end the largest company came to have a decisive influence on the lengthy and dramatic political process. Some radical changes in the local organizations were made a prerequisite to tackling the other changes necessary. At this stage the conflict with the small members became acute.

The problems described here can appear in various guises. Take the case of the Provincial Savings Bank. The organization had originally been set up to help promote the economic interests of the local community and this, as we have seen, also became one of its major external goals. Over the years, however, the government body set up by the parent came to represent a powerfully conservative factor, obstructing the formulation of new and more realistic external (and, to a great extent, internal) goals.

The successful leader of an institution has to develop considerable political skill. He should have ample personal authority and access to the instruments of power. But in this respect he faces the same problem as the leader of the corporation: if his power is too great, he may risk losing—or never gaining—other supporters for his organization, either inside it or outside. It is often greatly to the advantage of an institution to sacrifice a certain amount of its freedom. We have only to remember how much the Provincial Savings Bank owed to the confidence it had created by renouncing some of its freedom in favour of local trustees. It was also through its democratic structure that one of the Employers' Associations could effectively control its members.

> Karl Westlund & Co. provides an interesting example of a highly institutionalized private company and of the difficulties that it meets because the institutionalization is not reflected in the external and internal political structure. Faced with the need to change external goals, Karl Westlund found it difficult to engage even his closest colleagues. He had to solve the problem by a long process of education and some changes in key posts, and by gradually relinquishing his freedom of action (e.g. he tied his own hands in a series of pronouncements inside and outside the company; he made plans, cooperative agreements, etc.).

Thus, for the institutional leader, the only possible path is often to trust in his own ability and use his powers carefully to make the necessary changes in successive stages. First he may have to attack a political system that would otherwise obstruct the changes he envisages. In this he generally has to be very careful not to destroy more than is absolutely essential and not to provoke a revolution. Other useful tools are changes in key posts, the use of technical innovations, cooperative agreements, the utilization of other critical events that temporarily enhance his influence and, above all, what I have called 'joint consultation'.

Describing and Classifying Real Organizations—Some Examples
In the previous sections case studies and other empirical material have been used to illustrate isolated relations or typical cases referring to individual subsystems. In other words I have in general chosen to present the purest cases provided by the material available. Table 5:1 provides a summary of the characteristic features assigned to the four different cases. However, any reader who has tried to compose a picture of one of the organizations from the various scraps of information provided in various contexts above, will have found that the composite description by no means lends itself to classification as one of the ideal types.

Perhaps a few years ago the Provincial Savings Bank may have represented a fairly pure case of an institution; since then, however, it has taken on increasingly the character of a corporation while, because of its limited resources for the development of systems, it is also on certain

Table 5:1. Four ideal cases of consonance between subsystems and between organization and environment

	Marginal organizations	Appendix organizations	Corporations	Institutions
Value environment	Free value environment	Political value environment	Free value environment	Mixed environment
Task environment Production system	No categories have been suggested with regard to organization types. Concrete cases of consonance and dissonance between task environment and production system have, however, been given			
Value system (goal system)	Neither external nor internal goals	External goals	Internal[a] goals	External and internal goals
Value-supportive systems (especially power system)[b]	Total centralization of power	Centre of power: principal	Management enjoys limited centralization of power	Centres of power: management and environmental groups that support the organization
Defence systems (especially political system)[b]	Relatively weak defence system does not obstruct freedom of action	Often used to protect the organization from the principal	Relatively strong defence system contributes to stability	Defence system often complex: coalitions between parties in the organization and legitimatized power centres outside
Administrative system (cognitive system)	Good view of changes and chances in the task environment; 'nose for business'	Dependence on good communications with principal	Resources for system development	Resources for system development and for surveying the social scene
Processes for reaching consonance with the environment	Mapping	Matching	Dominance through system development	Joint consultation and joint optimization

a Often institutional quasi-goals (see Chapter 6).
b The relation between these types of system and the organization types have not been discussed in detail in the text. However, some examples of consonance and dissonance have been given.

markets a marginal organization. My description of the Service Company provides a fairly clear example of an appendix organization which has tried to free itself from its principal, but not entirely succeeded in doing so. Most of the industrial companies described enjoy a position of dominance in some product areas and on some markets; on others they have no control over events. Thus in certain contexts (i.e. regarding some products, or at certain periods) they could be classified as corporations, in others as marginal organizations. The various government organizations and agencies seem, if we consider their power systems and development resources, to fall somewhere between appendix organizations and institutions.

In conclusion I would like once again to emphasize the complex nature of real-life organizations and remind the reader that consonance between subsystems is possible in other situations, and not only in the four cases described here. With this purpose in mind I will conclude with a fairly full description of Karl Westlund & Co. Of all the organizations we studied, this one had the fewest problems. In other words the different subsystems had achieved the closest consonance.

Karl Westlund & Co. is a building and construction firm in the far north of Sweden. Its environment has been described in Chapter 2. The market for industrial building and construction is pretty close to the type we have characterized as a 'free environment', whereas the market for home-building exhibits norms and values that are more environment-oriented. In this environment Karl Westlund has grown from a very small company which 'took work where and when there was any' to a company enjoying a position of dominance in that part of Sweden. At the same time the company's goals regarding its own development have become increasingly specific. They have been expressed, for example, in a detailed 5-year plan that covers results, sales and production for the period.

We have also told the reader how in addition Karl Westlund developed external goals and norms of such a kind that the company was able to fulfil the various general social demands and local expectations that are made on a house-building firm. This means too, that the company has earned a very good reputation with the local authorities and with various cooperative and communal building organizations. The president has made sure, partly by the selective recruitment of like-minded colleagues, that his own social engagement has support at all levels in the organization.

We have already described in brief both the task environment and the production system of the company. Here we should also point out that by stepping up its system development (e.g. location, policy and expansion of resources for turn-key contracts) the company has adjusted to developments on the market and has even to some extent come to control at least the local market. This has been a major cause of its success in competition with other local building firms. It has also helped to prevent encroachment by the big nationwide building firms, although in this context the local strength of the company, resulting from its social goals, has meant more.

In the administrative system the resources allocated to system development have been successively increased. But here the company faces an awkward dilemma. Further increases in these resources are leading to a rise in costs which matches ill with the company's market. On the other hand, if resources for technical and administrative development are reduced, the company risks elimination by the larger organizations. This was the major problem, and only two alternative solutions had been suggested; to expand rapidly, extending company territory into the south, or to let the company become part of some larger building firm.

The power system of the company existed almost entirely in the person of the president. Apart from his formal position at the head of the company, the president enjoyed the power of majority ownership. Furthermore, his standing in the community and his other talents were one of the company's major assets. In this respect the company most closely resembled a marginal organization. As far as we could see, this concentration of power had not led to any very serious problems of motivation. Most of the top men had been with Karl Westlund & Co. for a very long time and identified themselves fully with the firm. This is probably why there were practically no political alignments or other defence systems. However, when the president's closest colleagues became aware of his plan for a radical change in the internal goals of the company, some of them found the whole idea very alien. On the other hand there was never an open break or an organized opposition.

Chapter 6

The Problem of Growth

Leaving the simplified ideal cases that we have been using up to now to illustrate our various concepts, and turning instead to the complex of problems in real-life organizations, we find one particular phenomenon that frequently recurs. It is generally referred to rather vaguely as 'the problem of organizational growth'. It includes problems caused by rapid growth and the equally common problems of stagnation. I do not intend to deal exhaustively here with the whole range of situations between these two extremes. Instead the following discussion should be regarded as an interim report on current research in our institute. As in the previous chapters, my chief aim is to make possible a description and analysis of conditions in individual companies, because the problem of growth, like so much else, turns out to vary enormously from one organization to another. In this way the following account will also provide an example of applying the frame of reference introduced above.

Why Do Companies Grow?

Starbuck (1965) has made an extensive survey of the literature dealing with organizational growth and listed a number of alternative and complementary explanations of this well-known and much discussed phenomenon. The ten most important are:

1. Organizational self-realization. 'If firms do not expand, they contract; they cannot stand still.'
2. Management's need of adventure and risk. They play the game for its own sake.
3. Management's prestige, power and security. As Parkinson has said, 'An official wants to multiply subordinates, not rivals'.
4. Executive salaries depend on the size of the company.
5. Profit—a controversial topic because of its importance as a motivating force and its relation to company growth.
6. Lower costs—advantages of scale.
7. An oligopoly market—maximum sales as a goal.
8. Monopolistic power—perhaps most common in certain types of non-profit organizations such as trade unions.

9. Stability—the larger the company the less need to put all its eggs in one basket.
10. Survival—if the company is large enough, it will gain eternal life.

I do not intend to examine or comment on these earlier research results here, nor shall I try to provide a full answer to the question: 'Why do companies grow?' On the other hand I will use the frame of reference presented above for reporting some of the experiences from our case studies that may serve to supplement existing literature.

The Problem of Motivation in Organizations without External Goals
In a mixed environment the organization that lacks external goals is in an awkward situation. It will be exposed to criticism from its own employees and from society. The corporation, which must strive to dominate its environment, will be in the worst difficulties: the striving for dominance will not be accepted as legitimate unless the organization can give an adequate reason for its efforts. The greater the opposition, of course, the more knotty the problem.

In a country like Sweden the opposition can sometimes be formidable: a relatively strong and well-equipped government, closely allied to the trade unions and supported by public opinion, is very ready to suspect large companies of working against the interests of society. Such companies will find it difficult to gear location and employment solely to the company's best interests. Their right to the free use of natural resources, such as water and air, will be questioned; they will be severely restricted in their use of communication channels for advertising and propaganda. And there will be counterdemands: they are expected to adjust their employment requirements to the needs of society; they must protect and develop natural resources as society deems fit; in their use of the channels of communication they must avoid exerting 'undue influence' or infringing society's right to use the mass media such as radio or TV for purposes other than advertising.

In the USA, where the balance of power between the large companies and their opponents is quite different, opposition has previously come mainly from employees. At any rate, the main concern of the corporations seems to be the problem of employee motivation. The most usual solution is the formulation of quasi-goals. Like external goals, these can act as a spur and a stimulus, although as goals they are not genuine.

Frederic R. Kappel, President of the American Telephone and Telegraph Company, expressed the problem particularly well in two public lectures which he gave in 1960 and which he devoted mainly to these very questions. I will report his argument in some detail and even use his solution as an example of the way in which corporations try to deal with these awkward problems by formulating quasi-goals, although I know that many

Americans are very critical of the real achievements of Mr. Kappel and his corporation.

> The goals of a business give the people who work in it the direction they need to increase their vigor and their strength. Unless the business sets demanding and exciting goals, it runs a heavy risk of losing vitality. This is an area where people in top management positions have special responsibilities, for there is a close relationship between a company's major goals and the decisions its officers are called on to make. If these goals and decisions fail to stimulate others in the organization, and set them moving and working in ways that build vitality, then there is something missing at the top. (Kappel, 1960, p. 37)*

Thus he states clearly that goals are needed to stimulate organization members. But the goals must make sense: in some way a man's daily tasks must be allied to something that is felt to be socially meaningful.

> Certain larger goals have particular value because they give meaning to other aims. In the Bell System, for example, it is an important aim to find a better way to splice a telephone cable, or a faster way to handle a telephone call. But the work we do to accomplish these things takes on much more meaning when we are moved by some deeper or broader purpose, such as the kind of job we want to do for the nation, the kind of business we want to be. The goals that build the future are the goals that establish these broader purposes. They relate the near to the far, the present to the future, the individual to the business, the interest of the business to the welfare of the country. So they have great social meaning. (Kappel, 1960, p. 38)

Kappel then indicates at least one of the paths by which he has sought a 'broader purpose'. But first he makes a clear declaration of faith, claiming that large companies are desirable in themselves because they represent a philosophy, an attitude, 'the American way of life'.

> We in business are doing more than earning profits. We are doing more than furnishing goods and services. We are producing more than material wealth. We are working to help build a political and social system different in important respects from any other the world has ever known. The lives of our heirs will depend in great measure on how successful we are. The countries of the world are watching our progress as a nation. The emerging nations of

* These extracts (pages 114, 115 and 116) are taken from *Vitality in a Business Enterprise* by F. R. Kappel. Copyright 1960 McGraw-Hill Book Company. Used with permission of McGraw-Hill Book Company.

Asia and Africa are looking for models on which to fashion their own growth. Our whole Western society in all its aspects is engaged in a decisive struggle with the power of an alien philosophy, one that would destroy everything we value. The challenge to us is to demonstrate that the initiative of free men can continue to build strength for the future that will assure the prospect of freedom. (Kappel, 1960, pp. 5–6)

Another argument claims that the company exists for the sake of the market and the customers. In this context profits are a measure of success. This argument is more intricate because it has to be shown that profits are in fact a reliable measure of customer satisfaction and that the products really are of some value. This is often rather difficult to do. But the status—and therefore the motivating power—of a product can be greatly enhanced by the claim that it serves 'a broad public' and that effort is required to produce it. Kappel refers to one of his predecessors, a man who succeeded in formulating goals that still command enthusiasm and loyalty. He describes Theodore N. Vail, President of the American Telephone and Telegraph Company from 1907 to 1920.

But his great achievement was that he envisioned a boundless future, foresaw what would be needed in order to drive ahead, and set others working according to his vision. I say 'vision' because he set goals that must at the time have been considered visionary, but which, as we see them now, have been largely achieved.

In effect Mr. Vail said: 'We will build a telephone system so that anybody, anywhere, can talk with anyone else, any place in the world, quickly, cheaply and satisfactorily.' He said it for years and he said it in many different ways. He said it in the face of staggering technical problems, when in fact the available technology was insufficient to permit fully satisfactory service even over short distances. To contemplate at that time the physical and human resources required to reach such a goal was a fantastic dream. Yet it was not an unrealistic dream. What was then foreseen is now do-able, and we are doing it.

The point here is that a goal that builds vitality and works for future success is not a wishful fancy. It is not a speculation. It is a perfectly clear statement that you are going to do something. I would say that part of the talent or genius of the goal-setter is the ability to distinguish between the possible and the impossible— but to be willing to get very close to the latter. Another equally necessary ability is to know how to set action going and what direction to give it. (Kappel, 1960, pp. 39–40)

Galbraith (1967) has pointed out that expansion and technical superiority are both quasi-goals which exert a strong stimulus on the large group of leaders that he calls the 'technostructure'. Some years ago the word 'efficiency' was a sharply emotive word with something of the same aura; now it has been replaced by 'innovation'. As Kappel has shown, the business leader is not usually content simply to formulate quasi-goals: he also tries to enhance them with some lustre of social usefulness. Some common battle-cries are: 'we must maintain industry's competitive strength', 'we must maintain and increase our living standard', 'we must create a framework for continued social progress'. In a confidential report an American firm of consultants cited the following as 'typical' goal formulations:

> To protect and sustain existing products and markets. To maintain the company's market share and financial stability. To improve its economic performance by developing new business capabilities thus making possible growth and profit ratios better than the average for all U.S. manufacturing industries.

We can see very clearly here the competitive spirit that often inspires the formulation of quasi-goals. In fact, and this seems to me a very interesting observation, companies seem to enrol themselves voluntarily in this type of competitive game. In formulating their objectives and goals, monopoly companies, public utilities, towns, municipalities, and government departments, all subject themselves to demands similar to those usually made by the market on the ordinary business enterprise. Kappel's formulation of a product development goal for the Bell System provides us with an interesting and typical example of this.

> So we have a new goal.

> I can describe it in a very few words. It is to give our customers the broadest possible range of choice in services available through our network, and I mean a range of choice that will be fully comparable to the choices or options offered consumers by nonregulated, competitive industry. Of course, we have no thought of stepping outside our proper sphere in providing communication services to the public. But our goal is to conduct our business in such a manner that our customers will see in the result, in our line of goods and services, all the virtues of competition, in addition to all the values of a single, interconnected service. (Kappel, 1960, p. 48)

I do not mean to claim on a basis of this example, that the company living a life sheltered from competition is as efficient in such things as product development as a company on an unregulated market. This may sometimes be so, but it is not the point I want to make here. What is remarkable is that the leaders of sheltered companies seem to design challenging goals reminiscent of the world of tough competition.

> The Development Company invited comparison with privately-owned companies. 'We must be at least as efficient as the private companies.' The Transport Administration Office often used similar comparisons. The following extract from the introduction to their long-range plan shows something of the competitive spirit: 'TAO is one of the largest companies in the country. It occupies a central position in Swedish society; its services are important to both industrial production and private consumers. However, the demands made on the organization, and technological developments in the industry, are both undergoing rapid change. Thus management must continually review the efficiency of present operations and plan the changes and development work necessary if the organization is to adapt successfully to a changing environment.'

Quasi-goals are sometimes bewilderingly like external goals. What distinguishes them from the genuine article is not their wording, but the way they are related to the value system and the value-supportive system. Quasi-goals are never tested. Unlike strategic or genuine social goals they are not examined and compared with alternatives. Since they are simply beautiful bits of phrasing—perhaps subtle rewordings of strategic goals— they need be tested only for effect: do they sound challenging? Managements are often fully aware of the need for disguise; quasi-goals are made to sound as much like real external goals as possible. Sometimes managements even succeed in deceiving themselves. The following are a few examples from our experience:

> In the long-range plan of one of the appendix organizations that we studied, the preservation of the company was specifically cited as a goal. It was justified on the grounds that the organization was a valuable asset to the country, being unique of its kind in Sweden. That this was a quasi-goal, distinguishing the strategic goal (perfectly reasonable in itself) of company survival, could best be deduced from the fact that it was not subjected to any test. The justification of the goal was never questioned. Might there not,

for example, have been an alternative way of preserving these same resources, or another way of using them for social ends?

I would also like to include among quasi-goals those which to some extent stem from a genuine interest in social matters, but which have not been fully developed and do not really govern the organization's actions. Typical examples are goals that govern various often rather far-fetched PR activities. Although they inspire a particular limited activity, I still classify them as quasi-goals because they are not otherwise integrated into the main value system. The interest of the Provincial Savings Bank in preventive medicine is a typical example, although we acknowledge the president's genuine engagement in these matters.

The Construction and Building Company provides a more complex example. We worked together with the heads of this firm for about two years. Nevertheless we are still not quite sure whether the company interest in improving the standard of Swedish housing and making it possible for people to move from apartments into individual homes, stems from a genuine external goal or whether it is a quasi-goal coined for the purpose of motivation.

During its 15-year development period the company has tried everything from the production of refrigerators to the building of power stations in Egypt. The capital acquired by various successful operations has generally been lost by operations in some other sphere. A few years ago, however, the structure of ownership and management underwent a radical change. The new management is fully determined that in future the company must develop in a more planned and goal-oriented way. Because of connections with a large and financially strong investment company, management sees no reason to reject an ambitious goal as unrealistic. Indeed, in view of the expectations of the investment company, it even appears necessary. It is hoped that the company will attain a leading position in the industry—even, in the long run, in Europe. But, while cherishing these grandiose but vague plans, management is also seeking external goals. In this search the president (who is still a minority shareholder) is particularly keen. 'A high return on investment' is not for him a sufficiently meaningful goal: the present company and the one that he dreams of must be the means of achieving far more significant aims than this. Gradually the Swedish housing problem emerged as an area that did seem to promise a worthwhile goal.

Growth as Protection against Future Threats

By letting growth become a kind of replacement for genuine external goals, the managements of corporations in a mixed environment try to satisfy society, and in particular their own employees, that their company's ambition to develop itself further is justified. Long-range plans are a great help here, because the longer view of company activities often serves to emphasize that present conditions (as regards products, markets, production processes, etc.) are of limited duration and that new tasks must be sought now. Our experience suggested that such a view did more than any other single factor to persuade management that growth was the only alternative. One of the few similarities between the various long-range planning projects in our material was that, after setting aside some time over a period of a year or more for a systematic discussion of the future of the organization, all the management groups concerned became aware of the threats and the new opportunities which that future could be expected to bring. And, since there seemed no point in waiting until the rot had started, the only possibility was to expand at once.

When we were working together with the Development Company, the organization was having great difficulty in finding time for its current work programme. Nonetheless, in view of an expected decline in the main sphere of operations, a decision was incorporated in the long-range plan to engage immediately in various new areas.

The Registration Office was burdened with an overwhelming backlog of pending applications. At the same time it was under considerable pressure from the Ministry to reduce personnel. Nevertheless, when in the process of the planning the heads of the Office became aware that the situation could change even within the next five years, new tasks were brought up for discussion. Plans were considered for the gradual development of an extended technical information service.

Developments at Karl Westlund & Co. were even more dramatic. When we first came into contact with this company, management was full of confidence, ready to use the present good times to embark on long-range planning. Six months later the same management was plunged in the deepest despair. They realized that in a few years time their market would begin to shrink; it was not easy to see a way out of the difficulties. Another year's hard work was to pass before a new path could be found and the company regain its confidence. The new plan included ambitions for rapid growth.

In some ways, perhaps, organizations are like runaway trains. And yet the simile is misleading. When an organization is travelling over rising ground, it increases its speed to be sure of getting over the top. And of course it cannot help accelerating on the downward slopes too.

Growth Is Not Always a Goal

While the problem of the corporation is—and perhaps, even more, will be—to get growth accepted as an external goal and to prevent its 'quasi' nature from being detected, many appendix organizations and institutions suffer from another, often more serious, problem. In many organizations of this type we found a strong tendency towards growth, even though this was not consciously sought after. In fact, in the various public agencies that we studied—the Transport Administration Office, the General Hospital, the Registration Office, the National Rationalization Office and others—we even found that one of the major internal goals was to avoid the growth that the external goals seemed to make inevitable. The organizations each formulated the problem somewhat differently.

TAO was not aware of having too much or too little staff. On the other hand the organization was faced with the problem of the efficient use of growing economic resources. Because of this it was envisaging a gradual change in personnel structure: certain types of qualified personnel were going to be needed in greater numbers.

At the Registration Office and in the General Hospital internal planning was haunted by the necessity to inhibit growth. For a long time both organizations had been growing, particularly since the war; both still found it difficult to satisfy external goals; as far as possible both were struggling to limit the number of clients awaiting attention.

The situation at NRO was rather different. Management was convinced that certain parts of the organization must be given the opportunity to expand rapidly, but realized that this was impossible within the present organizational framework. It was also felt that other operations could be reduced, while raising the quality of the personnel.

Even in the industrial companies that we studied, we often heard voices raised against the suitability of growth as an external goal. Criticism was particularly sharp in the two building and construction firms and in one of the cooperative service companies. In the building firms, for example, we often heard talk of 'turnover sickness'.

Conclusion

By these examples I have tried to show that there is no simple explanation of the fact that organizations so often tend to grow. On the other hand it is clear that while in some cases a number of factors conspire together, in others the situation is more complex. We can expect to find the strongest ambition towards growth in corporations, without external goals and operating in a mixed environment where growth is accepted as a substitute for other goals.

Mechanisms for Growth

Experience from our case studies suggests that the process which in accordance with common usage I have been calling organizational growth, can best be understood after a more detailed analysis and a division into two subprocesses. One of these is in the nature of a learning process, implying that a new and more complex structure is developed inside the company. This can be accomplished by using one of the mechanisms for achieving consonance described in Chapter 2, namely, mapping, matching, or joint optimization and joint consultation. The second subprocess involves the extension or enlargement of the company, usually through the domination of new elements in the environment. The two processes are often combined in one complex process which I will now try to describe. My presentation refers chiefly to conditions in corporations.

The Company's Territory

The company's strategic position has been defined above as its role (i.e. its exchange relations with the environment) and its resources (technical, economic and personnel). The part of the environment which the company dominates will here be called its territory. This territory plays a major part in the company's growth.

In our case studies we found examples of organizations which dominated one or more types of raw material source, and others which dominated one or more submarkets. The main examples of the first kind are to be found in the mining, oil and forest industries. Many of Scandinavia's present-day forestry companies were established several hundred years ago in the neighbourhood of iron-ore deposits. To be able to work the iron-ore, charcoal was required. For this reason these companies also acquired large tracts of forest. Gradually the forest resources came to represent the raw material territory around which the companies developed. It is interesting to note that companies with very large forest resources have remained raw-material oriented longer, while those whose raw material territory was smaller were forced to integrate forward at an earlier stage and, by specializing or in some other way, to try to achieve a dominating position on some kind of product market as well.

Nilsson and Svensson was the most profitable of all the companies we studied. Nor had any other company so consistently applied,

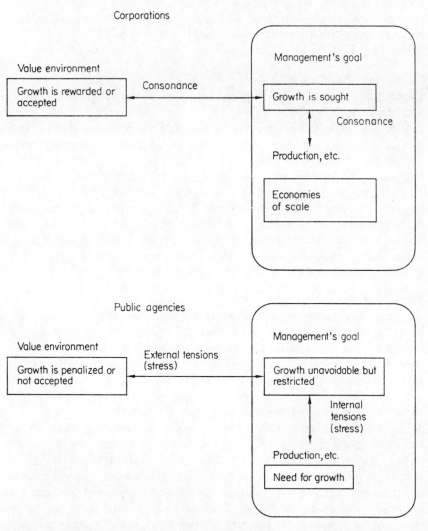

Figure 6:1. By prescribing growth as a substitute for external goals, corporations can achieve consonance between different internal and external subsystems in a way that is not always possible for other organizations

and succeeded in carrying through, the principle of dominating its environment. Operations were concentrated in one of the most rapidly growing metropolitan areas in northern Europe. Here, by means of a farseeing series of land purchases, the company had managed to obtain control at an early stage of the most valuable deposits of an important raw material (and one which was difficult to transport) required for one of its main products. However, this was not all; quite soon the company also began to use some of its extensive profits for the creation of an efficient and conveniently located production and distribution apparatus. Unlike most of its competitors in the industry, the company was also very ambitious in building up a sales organization. Certain important private and municipal customers, in particular, were carefully cultivated. The company dominated, in its areas of operations and on the relevant product markets, both the raw material supply and the market.

The simplest way of determining, at least provisionally, whether a company has a dominating position on a particular submarket is to group its sales according to products and geographical areas or customer groups, and to attach to each figure thus arrived at an assessment of the market share and a suitable measure of profitability. It then appears that in general profitability is greatest in connection with those products and markets where the market share is over 35%. If we let these market segments represent a first assessment of a company's territory, it often seems as

Market / Product	Italy	France	Finland	Denmark	Sweden	Norway	West Germany	England	Holland	Rest of Europe	Other exports
A	0	0	0	0	1	1	1	1	1	0	0
B	1	0	0	2	3	1	3	1	0	0	0
C	0	0	0	0	0	4	1	0	0	0	0
D	1	3	0	1	4	1	0	0	0	0	0
E	0	0	1	3	3	1	1	1	0	1	0
F	1	0	0	0	4	1	0	0	0	0	0
G	0	0	3	4	0	0	1	1	1	1	0
H	0	0	1	3	0	1	1	1	1	0	1
I	0	0	0	3	0	3	3	0	0	0	0

Figure 6:2. A European industrial company's territory (the figures represent different market shares as follows: 0=up to 1%, 1=1–10%, 2=10–25%, 3=25–50%, 4=50% or over)

though companies do not achieve high profitability until at least 50% of their sales come from their territory. Naturally this is only a rough estimate, based on limited material.

Feelers and Penetration Campaigns

A highly profitable market naturally invites competition and most companies regard it as an important part of their strategic planning to take steps to defend the territory they have acquired. Control of raw materials can generally be achieved by purchase or concession. Control of markets can be protected by product development, expansion of the sales organization, and implicit or open agreements about the limitation of competition. That companies behave in this way is a well-known fact which has been well documented.

Of greater interest both theoretically and practically was what we learned in the course of our case studies about the way companies behave when extending their territory. The most aware of them seem to argue more or less as follows: Control of our territory gives us, in the short run, the security and profitability that we need. But we want to push on from this base, systematically putting out feelers into new geographical markets, new product areas, or new technologies. These feelers must be designed so as to teach us as much as possible. It is therefore important not to evaluate them in terms of short-run profitability but in light of the new knowledge they can bring us. Such feelers must therefore lead to a decision either to renounce a particular market or to try to capture a dominating position (to penetrate the market).

While the basic aim of feelers and development projects is to collect new knowledge and superior solutions to environmental problems, market penetration consists of the invasion of a potential area of dominance with

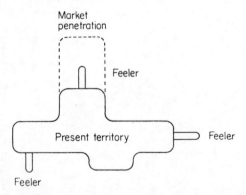

Feeler: Systematic investigation of new markets and technologies

Penetration: Systematic conquest of a dominating position on a market

Figure 6:3. Feelers and market penetration are two steps towards the conquest of a larger territory

the help of the superiority thus acquired. As was suggested in Chapter 5, the organizational structure within which feelers and development projects can operate effectively are essentially different from the type of structure which is successful in carrying out penetration campaigns. To use the terminology suggested by Burns and Stalker (1966), we can say that an organic or highly informal structure, with encouragement of individual initiative and entrepreneurship, is best suited for projects whose chief aim is learning and development. For penetration projects, however, a traditional military or mechanistic structure is more likely to be successful.

Principles for System Development

As was mentioned in the previous chapter, our material suggests that the successful conquest of a territory is often achieved by means of some kind of systems development, in which certain general principles usually seem to be applied.

One such principle or strategy, employed by many companies with great success, is the 'follow my leader' principle. Expressed in the terms we have been using, this means imitating a system developed by some other organization. The leading position of the other company is accepted; in the home company lower costs compensate the lack of standing. Sometimes attempts are made to surpass the leader in perfecting the system. 'We try harder.'

> Development in the Interior Decorating Company provides a good example. To begin with this company dominated its environment, but other companies followed its lead and imitated its system. By 'trying harder' the others have caught up; all the organizations in the trade must now be described as marginal.

Another type of strategy for system development is based on the discovery of some dissonance between the dominating organization and one of the subsystems in the environment. This is traditionally known as market segmentation. The competition between Control Data and IBM provides a well-known and successful example of this type of strategy. One of the Interior Decorating Company's competitors has also been particularly successful in its use of market segmentation.

> By identifying a rapidly growing segment requiring much higher product quality, a competitor has come to represent a very serious future threat. The Interior Decorating Company has tried to counterattack by developing products specially geared to this segment. But colleagues, sellers, and customers have all reacted

negatively. They say that these products are 'not the company's line'.

A third strategy, which we have already discussed, consists of seeking advantages by extending the system beyond the traditional boundaries. IBM's enormous success probably stems chiefly from an early decision to deal in software as well as manufacturing computers. Advantages of scale and system development will be discussed further in Appendix 5.

A competitor of the Forestry Company has won a big advantage by its creation of a highly integrated distribution system. The Interior Decorating Company has seriously considered developing its own chain of retailers and, possibly, extending its system of direct advice to the consumer. Behind these suggestions we find once again the idea of consonance. Inefficiency, stemming from dissonance between the present system and its environment must be identified. As an alternative to developing a retail chain of its own, the Interior Decorating Company has considered investing in salesman training, to improve the coordination of product development and sales.

One of the most successful examples of the coordination of subsystems is Volvo's engagement in the insurance business in some countries. By improving coordination between product development (making the car), servicing (e.g. planning of repair work and wage system) and insurance (e.g. settlement of claims and tariff system), the company was able to make its customers a really attractive offer.

The larger and the more closely integrated the system, the more important is the position of dominance. A classical example is that of the railroad companies: their success was remarkable so long as they dominated their environment, but when they lost this position to new system solutions (automobiles, air travel, etc.), they were rigidly committed to their own production system and unable to adapt.

The Forestry Company was in a similar situation. Until 1950 the company dominated its market. After that, because of growing competition from overseas and for other reasons too, the situation changed. Nevertheless, the company felt compelled to make big new investments with a view to modernizing and expanding its production. There was not always much hope of satisfactory profits, but there did not seem to be any alternative.

A fourth strategy consists of trying to change an existing system in some radical way, often by shifting its boundaries and/or introducing a new technology. This is often described as the search for a new 'concept'; its equivalent in military strategy could be the introduction of a completely new principle for warfare in order to retrieve an adverse situation. Levitt (1960) has pinpointed the essence of this strategy: an organization must be fully aware of the 'business' in which it is now engaged and of the 'business' in which it wants to be engaged in the future.

Any such attempt to achieve dominance over the environment by redefining the exploitable system is more likely to cause conflict with other organizations than a simple extension of the system. After all it means staking a claim to territory that cuts right across the traditional hunting-grounds of others. In Sweden the charter travel organizations have clashed with travel agents, air companies, bus companies and hotels. SIAR, the research institute behind the present study, bases its operations on a new system which combines research, education and consultation. As a result there has been a tendency to clash with educational institutions, the universities and ordinary consultant firms.

Any radical redesign of systems or system boundaries thus has its risks: but there is also much to be gained. Below we suggest three guiding principles for such redefinitions:

4.1 Construct the system to maximize the benefits of integration: do not include any subsystem unless it offers some important advantage.

4.2 Seek maximum uniformity of territory; otherwise some parts of the environment may not harmonize satisfactorily with the new system. This would invite competitors to conquer part of the territory by segmenting the market.

4.3 Investigate the risk of anyone else trying to conquer any part of the system by integrating it in some other way. System ideas that seem full of promise sometimes prove quite impracticable because it is not possible to incorporate one or two essential subsystems.

Internal Restrictions on Growth

Now that we have discussed the driving force behind company growth, and made a closer and more concrete analysis of the actual mechanisms involved, I would like to mention some other factors which also have to be understood before the development process in a specific case can be explained. These are in the nature of restrictions and are to be found both in the organization and its environment. We can start with the first type.

Leadership as a Scarce Resource

Our case studies showed that one overwhelming factor inhibits expansion. As a result, long-range plans are often too ambitious and cannot be fully realized. This important scarce resource is leadership. The groups we studied were generally better at making plans than at carrying them out.

Product ideas, expansion projects, decisions to enter new geographical markets, the establishment of a foreign subsidiary—all these are examples of decisions that a group can easily make, and with reasonably well-trained leaders the implementation of such plans can arouse great enthusiasm.

But leaders vary enormously when it comes to carrying out plans. At one end of the scale we find leaders and groups whose skill at explaining why they couldn't achieve a goal or accomplish a project knows no bounds, at the other end are the groups which from the beginning are determined to succeed. They get a firm grip on a project; they are unbelievably inventive in adapting goals and means to the desired end. In fact often the end finally achieved is even more ambitious than any plan had dared predict. Votaw (1964) has given us a vivid description of a leader of this type, namely Mattei, the creator of the Italian oil company ENI, one of the most rapidly expanding companies in the world during the post-war period. Votaw's account of the laying of pipelines (without the necessary legal backing) from the methane fields of the Po valley to the industrial areas of northern Italy is particularly enjoyable.

> Italian law had no provision for the condemnation of rights-of-way for pipelines; consequently any company seeking to provide pipeline transportation for the production of its gas fields was faced with the appalling task of negotiating contracts with thousands of small land owners and dozens of local governments and municipalities. Attempts to build pipelines in this fashion probably would still be in the negotiation stage. Mattei built the pipelines first and negotiated afterwards. His personality, his nationality, and his immense public reputation made it possible for him to do what nobody else, and certainly no foreign company, could even have attempted. Legends abound in northern Italy on how Mattei built the pipelines. The theme is the same in all of them: Mattei simply ignored private and public rights and the law. He boasts of having broken 8,000 ordinances and laws, and this must be a very conservative figure. Much of the work was done at night on the theory that by morning the work would be so far along there would not be very much that anybody could do about it. Once the ditch was dug, the pipe laid and the ditch refilled, the wound was not usually a very impressive one. When serious opposition arose, Mattei often appeared on the scene himself, full of apologies for his line crews who had 'acted in error and without instructions', but 'wouldn't it be a shame to have to dig it all up now?' The mayor of Cremona is reputed to have awakened one morning to find his town bisected by AGIP's nocturnal ditch digging and traffic completely paralysed; he was so glad to get

traffic restored that he agreed to rights-of-way on the spot. Mattei not only found the gas, but he also built the pipelines, and it is doubtful if anybody else, at that time, could have done the same. (Votaw, 1964. Originally published by the University of California Press; reprinted by permission of The Regents of the University of California)

This anecdote, which is only one of dozens, is about a man who in 1947 was asked to wind up a small, decrepit state-owned company. Fifteen years later he had instead of this company created an industrial empire with 50,000 employees and assets worth hundreds of millions of dollars. And this sort of leader, albeit on a more modest scale, was also to be found in some of the companies that we studied. Perhaps the most obvious example was the head of Alpha. As a result of this man's enormous inventiveness and drive, a decision to merge the three employers' and trade associations was pushed through.

In the small group appointed to investigate the possibility of a merger, the head of Alpha generally seemed set on finding solutions while the others, in particular the head of Gamma, concentrated on discovering problems. Member reactions, tax problems, internal organization problems, the reaction of the environment— according to the pessimists practically everything was against a merger. Most meetings ended in anxious mood. But before the next meeting the head of Alpha would have found time to seek expert advice, he would have discussed matters with members or collected other fresh material, he would have written a report and was ready to present the group with a solution. This skill in tackling obstacles was combined with an incredible eye for detail. The final decision was to be made at a joint annual general meeting for all three organizations. Naturally the 'real' decision had to be made beforehand; all unforeseen discussion must be avoided. During these preparations the head of Alpha emerged as an excellent 'producer'. The order of the speeches was carefully planned. Anyone who might be expected to have anything to say was asked if possible to submit a copy for examination beforehand. Colour slides, decorations, placing—everything was carefully planned.

Naturally much less has been written about the type of leader whose skill lies in explaining away his failures. Despite plentiful material, we too will maintain a kindly silence on this point.

Other Scarce Resources

The direction in which a system is developed in a particular industry will depend on several factors: the values entertained by the relevant environment, the special difficulties prevailing, the whereabouts of the main weaknesses in existing systems, and the current opportunities for technological development. From this follows the well-known fact that the subsystems of an organization are of varying importance. As Barnard (1938) pointed out, every organization has a strategic or limiting factor. The following are some examples based on our material.

> A research organization could achieve dominance by recruiting and keeping able researchers and/or by creating an internal administrative system geared to maximum utilization of the most creative members. A house-building firm could base success on a superior system of financing. A political organization with a new method of influencing political opponents would be in a very favourable position. A bank which integrated its own 'bank system' satisfactorily with the payment system and liquidity planning of its customers would be in a very strong position vis-à-vis its competitors.

We also found several examples of the converse situation: new product ideas cannot be used unless some means for producing, distributing and/or administering them can also be found. The partly state-owned Development Company, particularly, provided several examples of this. When the members of management became aware of the problem, they could see only one solution: to try to sell their own product ideas to other companies with better resources. But even sales of this type had to be systematized as an extensive network of contacts was needed within the organization and with the other companies involved.

Research and development resources are particularly important to companies which can—or are trying to—dominate their environment by means of superior system constructions. And naturally such resources must be matched by other resources (penetration resources) for carrying out any acceptable system solutions that emerge. For instance, a company that hopes to dominate its environment by the superiority of its production resources must have sufficient funds available to finance the necessary investments. It is interesting to note that, in several of the companies we studied, this—the financing side—was one of the weakest links in system development. It seems as though the people concerned are too bound by existing institutions, regulations, etc. to be able to make any creative innovations.

Resources for improving, modifying or diversifying products are essential to a company trying to dominate a given product area, but they usually have to be combined with other resources for marketing, technical servicing, distribution, etc. If resources are available for the development of new products, there must be other resources available for the construction of the necessary new systems of distribution, servicing, information and financing. Our experience suggests that the weakest links are not technical: most companies seem to have plenty of products and product ideas, but they lack the resources and ideas necessary for designing a system to identify and dominate a suitable market segment.

In this connection we noticed an interesting and important distinction between many American and most Scandinavian companies. Whereas American literature often speaks of the 'planning gap' in companies, meaning the unemployed financial resources, it seems to be more common among Scandinavian companies to suffer from a negative planning gap, i.e. there are insufficient financial resources for the market penetration required. This is probably because the profit-earning capacity of many Scandinavian companies is too low, with the result that their financial resources increase very slowly. Another important explanation is the emergence of the new larger markets: companies which have grown up in small markets, such as the Scandinavian countries, are now faced with a new set of requirements regarding the balance between investment in technological development and investment in market penetration and development. Since many Swedish companies have been accustomed for years to invest chiefly in technological development, many of them now find themselves with more products of international potential than they have the financial resources to exploit. Furthermore, at least until recently, mechanisms have been lacking for transferring large capital investments quickly from companies which are less capable of development to others better able to penetrate international markets. In my view, this is one of the chief reasons why some of the most expansive companies in Sweden, and to an even greater degree in some other European countries, have been bought up by American corporations and conglomerates which have been better able to understand and strike a balance between investment in development and investment in market penetration.

The main internal restrictions that sometimes prevent corporations from penetrating environments which would theoretically be open to them, are limited resources and organizational obstacles.

If the fire claims department of a large insurance company managed to develop a superior system for the quick and cheap repair of property damaged by fire, it is unlikely that the management of the company would be willing to allocate resources to a penetration of the world market, even if the inventors could prove that the return on invested capital would be greater than anything traditional operations could achieve. A cry of 'It's not our business' would be heard from all parts of the company, and people would point out the formal obstacles to an insurance company embarking on that kind of industrial operation.

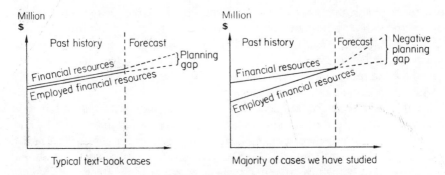

Figure 6:4. In small countries many companies face a serious problem in
the shape of financial restrictions on international growth
(the negative planning gap)

But a closer look at this type of argument often shows that it has a more
specific content. 'It isn't our business' frequently turns out to be nothing but
a declaration to the effect that if the company really did (successfully)
carry out such a penetration project, the balance of power in the company
would be completely upset, and a new management might even be necessary.
For this reason large organizations often countenance odd offshoots from
traditional operations so long as these have no real staying power. If they
have, they constitute a threat and will be rejected. The rejection generally
takes the form of a sort of informal expulsion, which is why many major
innovations have merged from small groups that have split off from large
companies (cf. Schon. 1967).

Even radical growth within the company's traditional area of operations
is likely to have far-reaching organizational consequences, and is therefore
difficult to implement. If a company grows to twenty-five times its original
size after penetrating the world market, it will probably be necessary to
replace as much as 80% of the top executives. This goes a long way to
explain why Swedish companies so often choose small and medium-sized
overseas markets rather than, for example, the American market. To hold
their own on the American market, they would first have to initiate a
thorough overhaul of the Swedish parent company's organization. 'When
a Swedish company comes up against a market of more than 12 million
people, management heads swim', said the marketing director of one of
the companies with which we had long and close contact.

In seeking a guarantee of success, large organizations often try to discover
systems capable of generating, developing and carrying out new system
ideas (systems for systems development). Sometimes their solution has been
the divisionalized organization structure (see Chandler, 1962, and others).
Recently, however, it has been suggested that this type of organization has

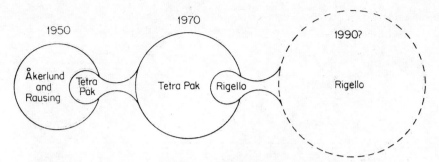

The chosen policy of a well-known Scandinavian packaging firm has been to split off innovation projects from the parent organization as soon as possible and to let them grow untrammelled. In most organizations, however, it is up to the truly enterprising to make the break from the restrictive parent on their own initiative.

Figure 6:5. Example of launching innovation projects

certain disadvantages (Tilles, 1966), partly because it cannot generate and embody within itself different kinds of system, and partly because the growth which it does generate tends to conflict with anti-trust legislation.

In recent years, two major innovations have been introduced which have radically increased the capacity of American corporations for system penetration. One is the *conglomerate* type of organization and the other is *franchizing*. Neither of these are in fact altogether new, but they have achieved a new significance as the external hindrances to system penetration (the heterogeneous nature of the environment and organizational obstacles) have disappeared.

The main difference between a conglomerate and a traditional divisionalized company is that top management in the conglomerate makes no attempt to attach to itself technical and marketing experts from the different subsidiaries' areas of operations. Central management is concerned only with financial and economic control, and coordination. The decisive advantage is that completely new branches of operations can be added and allowed to grow unhampered, or unprofitable operations discontinued, all without upsetting the balance of power at management level. In a traditional divisionalized company the central corps of experts often represents a serious obstacle to such a development. Because of its ambition to supply technical or marketing expertise, which is its only raison d'être, it is often extremely negative towards really new system ideas.

Franchizing is an organizational exercise which has lately become more frequent in the USA particularly in the service sector, with the purpose of penetrating the American and sometimes even the international markets. The usual procedure is for a parent company to hand over a fully evolved

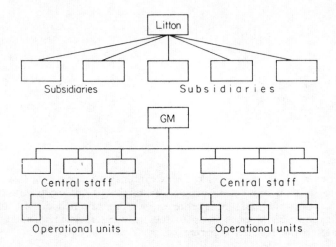

Litton and General Motors are prototypes of the conglomerate and the divisionalized company. Litton's management includes less than 100 people. GM's central staff must have about 3,000 qualified members.

Figure 6:6.   The conglomerate and the divisionalized company

system idea, and to supply all the requisite components, to a small independent entrepreneur. The latter must accept full control by the parent organization; its own main task is to provide capital, to bear the business risk, and to operate along the given lines. Restaurant chains, pizza bars, hairdressing saloons, and slimming cures are typical system ideas which have penetrated the American market by means of franchizing. This phenomenon is likely to appear more frequently in Europe during the 1970's.

The most successful organizational innovation to promote systems development is the informal cooperation that has sometimes been established between state and industry. The USA, for example, dominates several important technological spheres mainly because an extremely efficient form of cooperation has been established between private industry and the large military organizations. Together they form gigantic systems which dominate, altogether or in part, some major civil markets—sometimes on a world-wide scale. One or two similar attempts have been made in Sweden. For example, cooperation has been successfully established between L. M. Ericsson and the Telegraph Service for developing the telecommunication system, also between the State Power Board and ASEA for developing systems for the transmission of high voltage direct current. The role of the state in such partnerships is not simply to supply the necessary economic resources for development and experiments; often, and just as important, it is to provide the power necessary (often legislation) to implement experiments and any subsequent environmental adjustments.

External Factors that Determine Company Growth

One of the main insights we gain from comparisons between companies in the same industry in different countries, is that it is not only a company's internal situation that determines the rate and the manner of its growth. A study of this kind has been described in a report from SIAR (USA bygger, 1970) which emphasizes, among other things, the effect of the power situation on the way the different companies in an industry develop. For instance, because of the control of land exercised by the local authorities in Sweden, and the strong position of the trade unions and the architects in the USA, the building and construction industries of these two countries have assumed quite different structures. Below I will report some of the ways in which we found that external factors affect company growth.

Environmental Barriers

Our case studies were not generally of sufficient duration to enable us systematically to relate the companies' strategic decision making to environmental change. For this we have had to rely on historical studies. Nilsson (1971) has shown that the direction of a company's penetration projects depends on certain characteristics of the environment. Thus, after comparing the strategic development of two banking firms, and making a study of a brewery firm and the Swedish consumer cooperative movement, Nilsson found that these companies, which are all about 100 years old, have always tried to expand, either geographically or into closely related product areas, by applying a kind of law of least resistance.

Sooner or later expanding companies tend to meet some sort of barrier. The one-product company eventually discovers that it has conquered such a large share of the domestic market that it must seek other ways to expand in the future. But whether it decides to penetrate the foreign market or to introduce new products into its assortment, it is going to have to overcome a knowledge barrier. However, with the help of feelers, this problem can be tackled systematically, as has been described earlier.

Sometimes the barriers are more serious. In several countries banks are forbidden by law to operate outside a certain geographical territory, or to offer more than a rather limited assortment of banking services. In many countries insurance companies, breweries and transportation companies are subjected to strict rules of much the same kind. Custom duties, language problems, and different technical standards are other common barriers.

There is a marked tendency for companies to apply other strategies, rather than market penetration and system development, when they come

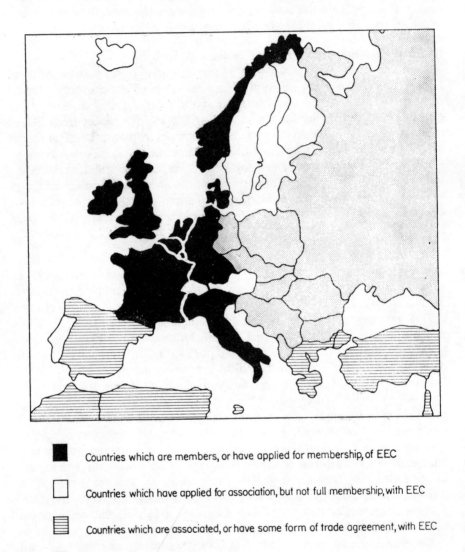

Countries which are members, or have applied for membership, of EEC

Countries which have applied for association, but not full membership, with EEC

Countries which are associated, or have some form of trade agreement, with EEC

Countries which are members of Comecon

Figure 6:7. The Common Market, together with the emergence of a commercial-TV network, has done much to remove the obstacles to system penetration in Europe up against serious obstacles of this nature. They are after all meeting obstacles that have been placed in their way, whether intentionally or not, by other organizations (the state, the municipality, trade organizations, other companies, etc.). Faced by such situations, a management's capacity for strategic thinking in the military sense is put to its greatest test.

In recent American literature there has been some discussion of strategy, in the sense of ways of defeating an opponent, which is of interest in this context. One firm of consultants, the Boston Group (cf. Tilles, 1966), has described various examples: a company conquers an opponent using the latter's funds for the purpose, or a company conquers another's territory and then frightens off any attempts at reconquest, etc.

Katz (1969) goes further and formulates a number of general principles for strategic behaviour; he divides them into those applicable to large companies and those more suitable to small ones.

In the first group we have:

(a) 'planning is crucial'
(b) 'give up the crumbs'
(c) 'preserve company strength and stability'.

The small businessman can learn much from guerilla warfare, says Katz, and suggests five important rules:

(a) 'attack when the enemy retreats'
(b) 'do not take full advantage of all opportunities'
(c) 'be as inconspicuous as possible'
(d) 'respond quickly'
(e) 'retreat when the enemy attacks'.

(R. L. Katz, *Cases and Concepts in Corporate Strategy*, Prentice-Hall, Inc., 1969)

In our own research material we have observed three strategies, which can be described in brief as follows:

(a) direct confrontation and exploitation of superior resources
(b) depriving the opponent of his freedom of action
(c) cooperating with the opponent.

If the barrier can be stormed in a confrontation using brute force, this is of course a fairly obvious solution. There were no examples in our case studies of international concerns being able to force any national government into removing an obstacle to market penetration. On the other hand we saw a corporation trying, unsuccessfully, to compel a local authority to remove the barriers it had set up for the protection of local industry.

Most cases of direct confrontation observed by us involved bigger organizations taking over smaller ones, for example with a view to gaining control over the latter's resources and territory (the expression 'to buy a market share' is very common in such cases). In this kind of financial strategical operation, the actual control of its own resources is not the only source of strength for the larger company. Particularly if its shares are dispersed and listed on the stock exchange, and the takeover can be implemented by floating a new issue, it has a splendid opportunity for mobilizing extra resources through a favourable quotation of its own shares. The company that manages to keep its price-earning ratio high can, by relatively slightly diluting the old owners' control, buy control of other companies with less favourable price-earning ratios. From the strategical point of view it is particularly risky for a company to have too great a part of its assets in liquid reserves. Particularly on the American market, but also to a certain extent in other countries, firms in this situation have been exposed to take-over, while the buyer company has financed the transaction wholly or at least partly from the liquid reserves of its new acquisition.

If the opponent's resources are in the same size range as the expanding company's it is often very uneconomical for the latter to try to force the barriers solely by exploitation of its own resources. In our talks with business managements we found rewarding material for discussion in the writings of a military author, Beaufre (1966), in particular his main thesis with regard to strategic thinking, namely that it is important to retain your freedom of action.

> A building firm which acquires large tracts of land can deprive a local authority of much of its freedom of action, particularly if the company itself can bide its time and direct its operations for the moment towards others areas (e.g. other municipalities).

> In the same way, by building up a valuable export operation which is also difficult to control, a domestic industry under threat of nationalization can deprive the national government of much of its freedom of action, at the same time increasing its own.

The least aggressive but often most successful strategy for overcoming a barrier to expansion is to initiate some kind of cooperation with whoever controls the barrier or with an organization on the other side of it. In various forms, joint ventures between private companies and government agencies have become more common all over the world. Similarily, American and European companies have found that a joint venture with a native company provides almost the only way of penetrating certain sheltered markets such as the Japanese or the Indian. We will probably soon be witnessing an increase in similar attempts at cooperation between western companies and companies in the Soviet Union or China.

On Competitors and Opponents

One of the most interesting things that we observed while collecting material for this report, with all the attendant opportunities for watching business leaders at work, is that the idea of 'opponents' is never directly acknowledged in company planning or thinking. We frequently felt called upon to remind business leaders that they are not alone on the market, that their competitors are also planning for the future, and so on. Our criticism was generally accepted, but did not often have any noticeable effect on further planning. This may of course be an example of genuine lack of forethought, but could there also be another explanation?

Naturally there is some awareness in all planning that customers, suppliers, creditors, state, and municipality are all affected in their evaluation of a company by the alternatives available to them. All types of organization have to face competition.

> The partly state-owned Development Company was hit hard by the efficiency of American companies in developing and marketing light water reactors. The Transport Administration Office had to compete with other agencies for the available investment resources. The problems of the Forestry Company stemmed mainly from the increase in production in non-European countries. The Provincial Savings Bank was hit by competition from other commercial banks and even from other savings banks. The management of the General Hospital complained that other county council districts were attracting young nurses.

But such contacts with competitors and other opponents were almost always indirect; and the rules of the game forbade countermeasures aimed directly at harming the enemy. The only permitted weapon was self-improvement: to develop a superior product or a superior system. Towards the market or the immediate environment, on the other hand, considerable aggressiveness was allowed: we have only to remember the Development Company's struggle for government appropriations, TAO's tussles with the local authorities, the Forestry Company's operations to finance an international project or the attempt at the Provincial Savings Bank to develop new products.

Are social norms, forbidding direct aggression against competitors, a sufficient explanation of this attitude or can the phenomenon be explained in any other way?

One explanation might simply be that it pays to leave competitors and opponents in peace and instead to concentrate on the market, which is full of unrealized opportunities. It is not necessarily difficult to find new products or new systems; what is difficult is to perfect a system that can exploit the product idea to the full. Moreover the market seldom takes revenge, as a competitor would probably do if faced with direct damage or theft. In this respect the market is fairly passive: at the worst it will refuse to accept an offer made by a company. This argument emerges more clearly if we look at the few examples in our material where direct attacks were in fact made on an opponent.

(a) The Development Company was exposed to direct attack from a government agency and from an industrial company. Both the aggressors claimed that the company had encroached on their joint territory.

(b) The Provincial Savings Bank found itself in acute conflict with another savings bank following the annulment of an earlier agreement concerning market shares. Big changes on the market had put the other bank at a disadvantage.

(c) At one stage in the negotiations for a merger between Alpha, Beta and Gamma, the last-named felt itself directly threatened by the other two. It was afraid of being swallowed up if Alpha and Beta, with their superior economic resources, were allowed to enter its territory.

(d) At an earlier stage in its history the Construction and Building Company had clashed seriously with the biggest firm in the building and construction trade. With a completely new product to sell, the Construction and Building Company had entered the market traditionally regarded by the other firm as its own. The big firm thus found itself in an awkward competitive situation. The behaviour of the Construction and Building Company was publicly condemned in the strongest terms; the head of the company lost his standing as one of the leading figures in the industry and it was many years before he regained it.

These examples indicate what is perhaps the most important explanation, namely that companies tend to fight tooth and nail to defend what they regard as their legitimate territory. Since, at the same time, they see the market as an environment full of opportunities, where it is mainly a question of effectively utilizing the chances offered, they rather naturally avoid direct confrontation with competitors and other opponents.

This tendency of organizations to define a territory and, as far as possible, to respect the territory of others, is something we noted in retrospect. I therefore lack material to support an explanation. Perhaps the whole attitude is no more than an expression of man's—and management's—instinctive need for a hunting-ground of his own.

I have taken the liberty below of changing two words in a passage from Morris' well-known book:

> Animals fight amongst themselves for one of two very good reasons: either to establish their dominance in a social hierarchy, or to establish their territorial rights over a particular piece of ground. Some species are purely hierarchical, with no fixed territories. Some are purely territorial, with no hierarchy problems.

Some have hierarchies on their territories and have to contend with both forms of aggression. [Managers] belong to the last group: [they] have it both ways. As primates we were already loaded with the hierarchy system. This is the basic way of primate life. The group keeps moving about, rarely staying anywhere long enough to establish a fixed territory. (Morris, 1967, p. 146)

The Principle of Systematic Suboptimization

I have suggested earlier that system development—to gain advantages for the corporation—must be directed mainly towards such parts of society as are inefficient, perhaps because coordination between components and subsystems is poor. At the same time the organization's own internal power system and society's power system both set firm limits on the corporation's efforts to press forward with a potentially superior system. The corporation which violates these principles will fail. One effect of this is that successful system development assumes something of the nature of a *systematic suboptimization*. To succeed, the corporation will have to limit its efforts to certain sub-areas where the profit to be gained from integration is likely to be great. At the same time, it will have to disregard as consistently as possible the effects on other parts of the system. This interesting phenomenon, i.e. that really successful system improvement can only be achieved by applying systematic suboptimization, is everywhere apparent. System development in the public health services is directed, for example, towards the industrialization of food production, but this is only possible by consistently disregarding the effects on the rest of the medical system. Improvements in the educational system are directed, for example, towards mechanizing the delivery of lectures through television, but this appears meaningful only if we consistently disregard the effects of the measure on the rest of the educational services. The rationalization of a company's administration is directed towards creating a more efficient mechanized information system, which in much the same way is meaningful only if we disregard the effects of this on the company's long-term capacity for adaptation. By quoting these examples I do not mean to imply that all rationalization is meaningless or misdirected. I only want to point out that successful rationalization presupposes the isolation of a sub-area within which systematic suboptimization is carried out. Or, to put it more dramatically, the system developer who tries to take into account any effects on the environment outside the relevant territory will always end up the loser. If, for example, two restaurant firms or food industries are competing to supply a complete system of food production and distribution to a hospital, the system supplier who concerns himself solely with suboptimizing food production and distribution, will almost certainly be able to offer the lower price.

The Principle of the Leading Subsystem

To be able to understand the consequences of the principle of systematic suboptimization, we must first combine it with another observation. At any one time in a complex society there will be certain sub-areas where the potential for improvement (which depends partly on the initial situation and partly on technological developments) and the power system together act as a stimulus to particularly rapid development. Such sub-areas will steer developments, and around such *leading subsystems* a series of related changes will occur. Generally speaking we could perhaps claim that for a long period the consumer production industry was such a leading subsystem, while at the present time the distribution of goods and the information system are leading the transformation of society. Computer technology, the exploitation of television and telecommunications, the distribution of goods, etc. are all areas in which major contributions to system development are now being made.

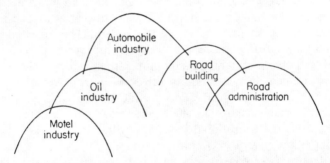

Figure 6:8.   The automobile industry has been a leading subsystem. In its wake several different system developments have been possible

The principle of system suboptimization and the observation that certain subsystems hold a leading position, together describe something that is already well known: that changes in society occur in waves; a local system development sets a wave in motion which in the end destroys a boundless area within the established order (Schon, 1967). Automobilism, computer technology, and petrochemistry illustrate three such wave fronts. Each started as a limited system development whose consequences spread ever more widely, but where every partial change occurred in accordance with the principle of system suboptimization. Automobilism called for the creation of the oil industry. In most countries road administration has become a major government operation. These developments in turn have created the construction industry, traffic safety operations, chains of subsuppliers to the automobile industry, the principle of assembly line production, the mechanization of the police force, the rebuilding of towns, etc. All this has taken place as a series of suboptimized system developments.

Chapter 7

Changing the Organization

Let us suppose that we are preparing to help the management of an organization. This was generally our intention, of course, in the case studies reported in the previous chapters, but perhaps now, after acquiring and systematizing our experiences in a language for describing the origins and solutions of organizational problems, we will have a better chance of making a useful contribution. In this chapter we will study the way in which a consultant with this experience, and with the arguments of this report in mind, could work. What limitations would he have to accept; what would be the risk of further complications and problems arising from his presence; what tools would he need? We will discuss first how the various ideas put forward above can be utilized in systematic consultation. We will then approach an even more difficult problem: how can consultants help the organization to change in the desired direction? It is, after all, one thing to know how a company could solve its problems, and quite another to transform these views into actual change.

A Systematic Approach—Diagnosis
The realistic consultant will not expect his job to follow a simple standardized pattern. Let us assume that, for some reason, an assignment interests him (perhaps because he believes in the importance of a solution for that particular organization). Before he can get to grips with the basic problems, he may have to do quite a lot of preparatory work. We often experienced this: in several cases we withdrew from assignments because we were unable to achieve acceptable conditions for our work.

> In one company, for example, we soon became involved in an internal conflict. Two parties were struggling for power. Since we failed to anchor the project firmly in the authority of the president, in which case it would have been raised above the struggle, we withdrew. Despite repeated requests from the client, we did not return.

However, although our fictitious consultant may have to follow a very winding path towards a goal that he never reaches, perhaps we can suggest

a few general rules of thumb that might help. For instance, it is probably
a good idea, as soon as possible, to collect information on which to base a
tentative understanding of the organization and its problems. The theory
and descriptive terminology that we have developed in the previous
chapters can provide a framework for the diagnosis.

Diagnosis : Preliminary Steps

Before embarking on a systematic diagnosis two preliminary steps are
generally to be recommended: to collect information about the history of
the organization, and interview anyone likely to have an opinion about
the problems—what they are and how they arose. Annual reports, anni-
versary publications, and persons who were present at the founding of
the company or at some other important stage in its development, are
likely sources of historical information. Management and representatives
of major environmental factions (stakeholders and other evaluators) will
probably have views on current problems.

> While working with the National Rationalization Office we
> carried out an experiment to test the reliability and validity of this
> type of preliminary measure. Five consultants were asked
> separately to carry out a series of interviews and to summarize
> and interpret their impressions. The five came to basically
> different conclusions, partly because they interviewed different
> persons, and partly because they started off with preconceived
> ideas that strongly affected the way they intepreted the inter-
> views.

One consultant classified the problems of NRO as basically the result
of rapid expansion. Another pointed out that NRO was expected to carry
out incompatible tasks. A third felt that management had failed to formulate a strategy and goals. A fourth declared himself unable for the time
being to come to any conclusion. This experiment provides a warning
against concluding too much from a preliminary diagnosis. On the other
hand, we could see at a later stage that a combination of all the first
impressions did provide a pretty good picture of the overall situation.

Structural Disintegration

The next stage in a systematic diagnosis should be to study more closely
the variations and disturbances inside or outside the system which are
threatening to break down its structure. Whenever such threats are discovered, an important question must be asked: can the organization maintain and, if possible, improve its structure despite the disruptive forces?
If not, it will disintegrate, as described in Chapter 1 and Appendix 2.

If the consultant has experience of similar organizations, he may be able to draw fruitful comparisons. Compared with these other organizations does this one appear to be well run, with reasonably well-defined roles and satisfactory routines? At the same time, too much reliance should not be placed on such comparisons: as we have seen above, structural changes in the environment can make great demands on a company's adaptability, which in turn can affect the stability of its structure.

Tools for measuring attitudes—to the organization, to bosses, to colleagues, etc.—can also be useful in helping to localize problems of structural disintegration. But here too comparison will probably have to be made with very similar organizations. As Burns and Stalker (1961) have shown, there will be more stress, more strain, and more conflict in an organization undergoing great structural change than in another that enjoys a stable environment.

The Impossible Environment

The next suitable step in a diagnosis can often be a general evaluation of the difficulties involved in satisfying the demands of the environment. There are, as we have seen, some environments that are generous and some that are less so; sometimes, in fact, it may be almost impossible for an organization to avoid serious problems (cf. Chapter 3). In particular we saw that during periods of rapid environmental change organizations are often exposed to such conflicting demands that, whatever their behaviour, they are sure to be criticized and may well be subjected to sanctions. The most interesting example of this in our material was the Development Company, whose situation could justifiably be called 'impossible'.

At this point, therefore, the main task is to examine the organization's value environment. Who are the evaluators? What demands do they make? How difficult is it to fulfil the demands? How serious are the sanctions available? The answers to these questions will supply valuable information for the next step.

Consonance between Value Environment and Goal System

The next step, probably, will be to find out whether or not the goal system of the organization is in harmony with the value environment. This presupposes the existence of a method for identifying the value system of the organization—something which is difficult to do and which we have only briefly touched upon. Here, however, are some methods that we have used in various combinations to obtain data about the internal value systems of organizations: to study the formal organization; to examine critical decisions in the organization's development; to investigate contacts with other organizations; to hold interviews with members of management.[18]

At the same time, if there is some dissonance, the consultant should try to explain how it has arisen. As we have seen in Chapter 2, there are generally strong forces working for consonance, which is the natural state; explanations should be sought for any deviations from the norm. If none can be found, perhaps wrong conclusions have been drawn about either the value environment or the goal system of the organization.

Consonance between Goal System and Other Subsystems

The last and often most laborious step in the diagnosis is to find out whether the goal system in the organization accords with the other supportive systems, in particular the cognitive system (information-processing resources) and the power system. There are two special difficulties here: first, the circumstances of a company at any one time rarely lend themselves neatly to classification as one of our 'typical' situations; secondly, according to the principle of equi-efficiency, demands can be satisfied in many different ways. Yet another problem is that certain structural conditions which appear at a superficial glance to satisfy the demands of the situation, may not in fact do so. How are we to tell? The existence of a development department, for instance, by no means guarantees that an organization can discover new systems; or perhaps an apparently successful management is unable to master political forces opposing a necessary change.

There seems no other way of tackling these difficult problems except through long and intimate contact with the organization. Only by studying, on the spot, how changes are actually made and what difficulties they meet, can the consultant decide whether the various subsystems are satisfying the demands of the situation. In practice the simplest approach is to make a preliminary diagnosis and suggest what changes can be expected. By clearly expressing his expectations already at this stage, the consultant commits himself to the probability of later modification of his diagnosis in the light of new information—an important step that he might otherwise neglect.

Table 7:1. Factors in the recovery of consonance and efficiency—An example

1.	Leaders who can prevent the company running off course
2.	Maintenance of company structure
3.	Strategic planning: territory is defended, frontiers possibly extended
4.	Planned change in value-supportive systems to achieve consonance with external environmental change
5.	Experiments to probe completely new environments

Diagnosis—Some Examples

To illustrate the suggestions outlined above, I will describe two of our own *ex post* diagnoses. It should be remembered, though, that these have been made after the event, and that the theory behind them was worked out as a result of these and our other cases.

The Service Company was concerned about its internal efficiency. We were asked to help in the planning of its improvement. The president found it difficult to survey all the development projects that were under way; he had an unpleasant feeling that many of his suggestions led to investigations but rarely to any actual changes.

The president was clearly uninterested in problems unless he had identified and formulated them himself. At the start we agreed to help in the design of a system for the selection, planning and follow-up of internal development projects; we also suggested that a firm of consultants should be called in to help with the work itself. This was done. In the course of our therefore fairly limited advisory activities, we became increasingly familiar with conditions in the company. Among other things we realized that since his appointment five years before the president had carried out a very heavy programme which had done much to rescue the company from a complete breakdown. The result was there for all to see: sales had risen and profitability improved; even more important, perhaps, production was more efficient, morale higher, services of a better quality, and so on.

But none of this meant that the problems had disappeared. If anything, they had grown. In the president's view the parent company—Charter Aircraft—was the major cause of the trouble. The parent seemed quite unable to formulate goals for the operations of its subsidiary. This was a serious matter since the Service Company certainly needed a strategy and internal goals of its own. At the same time the president could see the difficulties: the parent company was operating in a rapidly changing industry; planning its own development was a difficult task and planning for its appendix organization an almost impossible one. The only solution that the Service Company could envisage was to take matters into its own hands. Goals were formulated and the president opened negotiations with the parent company. The idea was to establish the obligations of the Service Company vis-à-vis Charter Aircraft and to regulate the economic side of their mutual transactions, after which the Service Company would be free to set up internal goals of its own. For reasons which the president could not understand, the parent company refused to agree to this arrangement and negotiations were finally broken off.

To describe the situation in our terms: the management of the appendix organization was unable to deal with the political problems in its relations with the parent company; it was also unable to achieve the joint formulation of goals that must exist if an appendix organization is to avoid serious conflicts.

At first sight the Interior Decorating Company is an extremely sound company. In its own line it is well known. Its plant, and the whole community where it operates, gives an impression of order and wellbeing. The president explains that the real problem is the supply of personnel. As a result of modern educational opportunities and urbanization, the recruitment of good skilled workers such as the company feels that it needs is already difficult; in the future it is likely to be a really serious problem. Having given this as his view, the president then asks for our opinion of the company's situation in general. After all, his own interpretation may not be the right one: it would be helpful to hear a general evaluation of the company's situation.

At a meeting a few months later it appears that the president is not altogether satisfied with the company's financial results. (The reasons for this have been reported in another context.) At the latest meeting of the board, it has been suggested that the apparently satisfactory financial situation is an illusion, depending chiefly on a high degree of self-financing accomplished in previous 'good' years. Return on investment, which is the only reasonable measure of success, is extremely unsatisfactory—about 1%.

The diagnosis is complicated by the fact that the organization possesses very little information about its environment. Admittedly it is manufacturing consumer durables, but it does not sell direct to the customer. Almost the only facts known about the market with any certainty are: the distributor system is in the process of structural change, competitors have successfully launched products of essentially different design; price elasticity is low.

Several decades ago the company effected an important financial innovation which at that time endowed it with a position of unchallenged dominance. The innovation involved a completely new form of cooperation between bank and company. In the following decades the idea was copied by several competitors. In fact, even during its most successful years the company never dominated the foreign market, mainly because of inadequate production and marketing resources.

Marketing is a major cause of controversy in the company. The board has recommended the appointment of a marketing director. Previously the company had two sales managers. According to one critical board member, who has tried to make himself fully familiar with conditions in the company, they were really no more than salesmen. 'And in any case', he has told us 'I think the real reason why it's difficult to get anything done about these problems is that the president doesn't know what marketing is.' The decision is postponed. The president says he first wants to obtain the agreement of his collaborators, and that anyway for the time being he can manage with a marketing consultant.

1967 is a critical year. Sales drop so much that the buffer effect of an order backlog is lost. However, before the company has to start cutting down production, economic conditions improve and there is an increasing flow of incoming orders.

Is it possible, from this information, to make anything like a reliable diagnosis? Hardly. But it should be possible to formulate a hypothesis which can later be tested. Although the company is relatively small, it has once commanded a dominating position in the industry. It also has clear-cut external goals: management is concerned to maintain local employment—this is even considered more important than financial returns. In fact, there are good reasons for classifying the organization as an institution. Such a description would also suit the president: although he owns the company, he is most concerned to take into the account the various forces at work both inside and outside before making any basic change in the organizational structure. This would mean seeking the source of the problems in two quarters: first, there is the demand for economic results that is not yet reflected in the organization's internal goals; secondly, there is a lack of consonance between various subsystems, probably chiefly in the shape of insufficient development resources. The absence of a strong and capable marketing director perhaps reflects ignorance of the environment, but there is probably good reason to suspect that this is not the only weakness. A closer examination of the development resources that once gave the company its strong position confirms that they are no longer anything like as remarkable as they were. In fact in this respect some competitors are probably better equipped.

Unresolved Conflicts—A Recurring Theme

The blankly neutral expression 'lack of consonance between subsystems' gives us a poor picture of the feelings that actually prevail in organizations with problems. Conflicting value systems in an organization often lead to the emergence of factions, in some ways resembling political parties, which fight against each other. A split in management on the question of goals and ambitions may completely inhibit the possibility of discussing import- ant matters without an outbreak of emotional wrangling. The disagreement between management's goals and ambitions and those of certain other groups in the company may be the result of an earlier struggle for leader- ship, and it may lead sooner or later to a 'purge'.

I can say, without beating about the bush, that inhibiting antagonisms of this kind were a recurrent theme in several of the companies that we studied. At the same time it should be emphasized that some of these conflicts possess one characteristic that distinguishes them from the type of conflict so often found—and sometimes intentionally implanted—in organizations between for example the production and sales departments, or between the market's conflicting demands for high-class products that are also cheap. What distinguishes this kind of disagreement from the really serious conflicts is that the latter are unresolved.

The unresolved or persistent conflict appears to arise—sometimes but not always—when an organization has no superior goal or equivalent effective mechanism for solving or limiting the paralysis or inefficiency that dissonance between goals or values can sometimes generate. Thus, in an organization with a strong management and well-defined goals, inter- departmental conflict is rarely a serious problem; even an open conflict between two groups within management can be relatively harmless if it is concerned with a low-level goal (e.g. investment in product line A or product line B), always providing the superior goals are unambiguous and enjoy unanimous support. But if the management group is weak or split, or if the superior goals are unclear, interdepartmental conflict can represent a very serious problem. As we shall see below, such unresolved conflicts are often also unrecognized, in the sense that those with the power and the opportunity to solve or reduce them are not fully aware of all aspects of the very complex situation.

Operational and Structural Conflicts

In the literature the idea of organizational conflict seems to embrace at least three quite distinct phenomena. Before going more deeply into our analysis we must therefore be a little more specific about the meaning of the concept we are discussing. To the business leader a conflict usually means some sort of antagonism between persons or groups: for him 'conflict' is often a term with highly charged negative overtones; it is something he wants to avoid at any price. Organization researchers, on the other hand, are nowadays inclined to give 'conflict' a much less emotional meaning. For them it signifies roughly an 'inability to come to a joint decision'. Conflict solution, in this terminology, becomes synonymous with joint decision making.[19] However, there is also a macro-sociological tradition which sees conflict as the clash of antagonistic interests which is an (inevitable) part of some social systems.

In this report I want to make a distinction between operational and structural conflicts. By the first I mean some temporary conflict in the interaction between two persons or systems, resulting from disturbances and/or variations in these systems or their environment. By structural conflicts I mean conflicts resulting from some unresolved incompatibility (perhaps stemming from different values). Table 7:2 below illustrates the difference between these two kinds of conflict.

In this report I am chiefly concerned with structural conflicts, although this does not mean that I consider operational conflicts uninteresting or unimportant. The efficient solution of operational conflicts is an important precondition for avoiding the kind of breakdown in the organization described in Chapter 1 (and discussed further in Appendix 2). Moreover it appears that the methods chosen by an organization for the solution of its operational conflicts often have a considerable effect, one way or another, on its structural flexibility.

Kematech, a vertically integrated chemical industry, with some sideline operations, provided an interesting example of operational conflicts which occupied management's attention so completely that no time was left for solving other problems, such as product development. Because of the integrated production system, any disturbance at one level of production was easily transmitted to all parts of the company. Furthermore, because of high capital costs, it was felt that capacity should be utilized as fully as possible and, since capital was in short supply, management was very keen to reduce inventories to a minimum. This made the company even more vulnerable to any disturbances in operations or any variations in demand. For various reasons no proper central production planning had been developed. A couple of the factories had their own planning departments, but these could only review a very limited part of the company's total production system and of course did not touch upon the very complex customer situation. Since the financial importance of customers varied considerably, the selling side was in a powerful position when it came to setting priorities. The marketing director, who had previously been financial director, came to act more and more as a moderator of conflicts and a high-level production planner, rather than concentrating on the development of products and markets.

Structural Conflicts Originating in the Environment
One of the main postulates on which the whole of our present analysis has been based, is that conditions and events at different system levels are closely interrelated. Our material illustrates this yet again, when we see that unresolved structural conflicts at one level in a company generally have their counterpart at either a higher or a lower level in the system.

Table 7:2. Examples of operational and structural conflicts

Operational conflicts	Structural conflicts
Temporary disturbance in production resulting in a change in order priorities and leading to conflict between regional sales managers	Japanese competition makes it necessary to apply different sales policies to different markets; this leads to conflict between regional sales managers
An epidemic leads to conflict between the hardest-hit clinics in a hospital and the other departments. The latter feel that normal medical services are suffering	Some medical developments advance more rapidly than others; some clinics find it increasingly difficult to manage without laboratories of their own. Continuous conflict regarding access to the central laboratory
New sales director, whose habits are very sophisticated, comes into conflict with the financial director on the question of expenses	Big differences in market conditions make it very difficult to apply the same rules for expenses to all sales sections. Continuous conflict, particularly with the building materials division
Two maintenance men fall ill, with the result that the others are badly overworked. Several serious conflicts with customers and with the sales department occur simultaneously	Successive developments towards increasingly complex electronic products make it necessary to have a more qualified customer service. Training of maintenance men and service engineers is neglected, with a growing number of conflicts with customers and between the sales and service departments as a result

Thus, conflicting demands from the company's markets, or perhaps from society at large, can create a kind of double-bind which radically reduces the organization's efficiency. The partly state-owned Development Company and the Provincial Savings Bank have already been discussed from this point of view. International Mechanical Industries (Inmec) is a more complex and therefore more interesting case.

Inmec was founded at the end of the nineteenth century by a north German shipowner. It developed, mainly in the period between the wars, into a diversified company producing a variety of high-class products. In the post-war period a very efficient sales organization was created, aiming mainly at direct sales to the consumers of domestic capital goods. When we came into contact with the company it had recently undergone 'divisionalization', on the advice and with the help of an American firm of consultants. In the company this reorganization was generally regarded as successful and necessary, but it had not solved the main problems. We held a few meetings with the corporate management and divisional heads, and a list of problems was drawn up. We had prepared the ground for this beforehand in a series of interviews, and discussion at the meetings was very frank. Among the chief causes mentioned were growing competition and difficulty in maintaining the company tradition of superior product development. Moreover, several of those present felt that the company was in an impossible market situation, and that it should exploit its technical knowledge to try to penetrate some new area where competition was weaker. The list of accute symptoms included:

Unsatisfactory profit-earning capacity.

Difficulty in penetrating the European common market.

Extensive and scattered operations outside the company's 'territory'.

The planning and control system did not work.

Middle management frustrated by slow growth.

Complaints of both muddle and bureaucracy.

Complaints of poor communications.

Complaints of vague policy/lack of strategy.

Several of the company's best men were leaving.

The board did not function satisfactorily; it met increasingly rarely.

Personality conflicts and a tendency to form parties.

Many unsuccessful development projects.

Poor profitability despite dominance on some submarkets.

After a fairly long period working together with the board of directors and management, we as consultants and management itself began to change our ideas. It seemed possible to trace all the symptoms mentioned back to two unresolved structural conflicts. First there was a lack of balance in the company between financial resources and a wealth of technical ideas at management level and in several of the operational divisions. This could be explained partly on the grounds that, unlike so many other German firms, the company had not had the opportunity to accumulate huge profits in the first decade after the war. Another explanation, though, was the need to penetrate the whole of the Common Market and to face increased competition from the U.S. and Japan. This was putting an increasing strain on financial resources. A second structural conflict also connected with markets, resulted from the fact that the different product divisions enjoyed very different opportunities. The company's trademark was well known chiefly in Germany: at least two of its product lines were unlikely to achieve any real successes outside Germany (with the possible exception of Austria and Switzerland). In the case of these products a natural line of development could be to let the company develop as a sales organization for products manufactured on licence or bought from foreign companies. For two other product lines the situation was completely different. Given sufficient financial resources, it should be possible for these products to achieve a dominating position on the world market (excluding the Communist countries). The situation as regards the fifth product division was not clear. The best solution might be to discontinue the line. But management had taken no account of these very different opportunities. Instead it was trying in every possible way to coordinate the five product divisions, to give them the same conditions and requiring of them the same profitability, the same utilization of the foreign subsidiaries, etc.

When these basic structural conflicts were at last perceived and acknowledged by management, it became possible to carry out changes which essentially improved the situation. First, one production division was discontinued and certain other measures were taken to make a substantial increase in financial resources. Secondly the company was reorganized and the central corporate management reduced to a very small group. The organization was then divided into two operational companies, one for the two product lines aimed chiefly at the German market, and one for the international products. Furthermore, certain measures were taken to assure the continued coordination of technical developments, which was the company's traditional strength.

Structural Conflicts Originating in the Management Group

However, structural conflict in companies can also be connected with some kind of split in the management group, and this may, as in some of the cases we studied, have its counterpart at board level. Our observations show a certain similarity with research results reported by Zalesnik (1966). Zalesnik found that internal personality conflicts among the leaders of an organization seemed to be a major cause of organizational conflict. We lacked sufficient data on which to judge this hypothesis but we felt, as a result of our own experience, that Zalesnik's arguments could—and indeed should—be applied to studies of company boards. In many cases it seems only too likely that a personality conflict at top management level has its roots in (or is aggravated by) conflicts at board level. These, in turn, may link up with yet other conflicts, perhaps arising from incompatible demands stemming from the environment. In real life these unresolved conflicts of external and internal origin often combine to form an intricately complex pattern, in which it would be wrong to try to see any causal relationship. If such conflicts are ever to be resolved, however, their existence must be recognized by those with the power to effect radical changes.

SIAR had worked together with the Family Corporation on various research projects, which is probably why we were called in to advise on an organizational problem. As the company expressed it: 'We would like the opinion of a scientific expert regarding an organizational structure suitable to the present phase of rapid expansion.' SIAR's research team undertook a series of interviews and collected economic and market data. As a result of this they could soon report the presence within the company of two conflicting parties. Profitability had been increasingly poor for five years or more. Each camp had its own idea about how this trend could be checked. A powerful technical director, with supporters in various parts of the company, demanded rationalization, a reduction in assortment, and personnel cuts. The 'market party', including several of the younger members of the company, supported expansion, higher sales revenues, better product development, etc. The research team noted that, as a result of the tenacity of these conflicts, management had more or less ceased to function as a group. Many complex decisions requiring cooperation between marketing and production simply could not be made. The problem was further complicated by a very big product assortment: the company dealt in heavy industrial raw materials, where competitive strength and profitability depended on efficient production and low costs, and consumer durable goods, where product development, market planning, and an efficient sales organization, were all of the greatest importance.

However, what surprised the research team most was that the president made no use of his great personal authority to sort out the organizational problems. 'The president is a pure technician' was an explanation frequently heard. It appeared from interviews with the president that he was fully aware of the problems and understood their nature. He also understood that the market party were advocating the only realistic course. At the same time he himself was closest to the leading man on the production side. Also on one point he was extremely critical of the market party supporters: in his view they tended to exaggerate the financing problem.

This conflict—on the one hand a realization that considerable expansion was necessary, and on the other a fear of becoming overdependent on outside capital and weakening the family's personal power—turned out to be equally strong among board members. But it was difficult to persuade the directors to recognize their own dualistic attitude: they pretended to be prepared to seek capital for immediate expansion, regardless of the effect on the power situation; but they were not prepared to support the organizational and other changes that would then become necessary. And the failure to make organizational changes also delayed the financial restructuring.

Methods for Solving Conflicts

Operational conflicts can be solved or reduced in a variety of ways. In Chapter 1 some examples were given from a large hospital. As a result of queues, overcapacity, variations in the quality of the treatment and, above all, cyclical planning, the hospital was able to rise every morning to cope with a new series of crises, despite all the disturbances and conflicts of the previous day. Kematech, described above, was reorganized and, among other things, a strong unit for the control and coordination of production was established. The most important task of this unit was to solve operational conflicts between the various marketing and production executives in the vertically integrated company.

Up to the present the most systematic study of these questions is that of Lawrence and Lorsch (1967). This is a study of the resolution of conflict (or, as they call it, integration) in a variety of companies in the food processing, the plastics and the container industries. Lawrence and Lorsch found basic differences between the efficient and the less efficient companies in all three industries. Their results for the three most successful companies are summarized in the following table.

Table 7:3. Comparison between methods of resolving operational conflicts in three efficient companies in three different industries (after Lawrence and Lorsch, 1967)

	Plastics	Food	Containers
Major devices for resolving operational conflicts	1. Integrative department	1. Individual integrators	1. Direct contact between managers
	2. Permanent cross-functional groups at three organizational levels	2. Temporary cross-functional groups	2. Managerial hierarchy
	3. Direct contact between managers	3. Direct contact between managers	3. Paperwork routines
	4. Managerial hierarchy	4. Managerial hierarchy	
	5. Paperwork routines	5. Paperwork routines	

(From: *Organization and Environment: Managing Differentiation and Integration,* by Paul R. Lawrence and Jay W. Lorsch (Division of Research, Graduate School of Business Administration, Harvard University, Boston, 1967), Table VI-1, p. 138)

Far less has been written about methods for solving or reducing structural conflicts. In my foreword to the present report I mentioned that the traditional approach of social psychological research and consultation, which persistently recommends power equalization as a precondition of farreaching structural change in an organization (cf. for example Bennis, 1966), is not supported by our experience.

For this reason we were particularly interested in Schon's idea that, when it comes to effecting organizational change, two quite distinct leadership styles can be observed (Schon, 1967). Schon claims that both the 'Great Man' and the 'resource-building educator' can bring about farreaching changes in an organization. The former does it by supplying a detailed vision of the new development and imposing it from above: selecting, pushing and inspiring followers at many levels. The latter tries instead to change interpersonal relations and create the conditions for innovation, training others to share the responsibility for change.

This is one of the areas where our own research is obviously far from complete, but where I would anyway like to make two important observations. First, it seems that business managements do not have anything like full freedom of choice in deciding which of the two leadership styles described by Schon they would like to use. This is partly because the necessary structural changes may to a greater or lesser extent call for changes in the power system. And the higher in the power system the rupture has to be made, the more necessary it is that the business leader himself acts as the 'Great Man'. The classic example will probably turn out to be Mao Tse Tung's cultural revolution, but the following table provides some more trivial examples from our material.

Table 7:4. Two types of structural conflict

	Examples of structural conflicts from our case studies
(A) which could be solved within the existing power system	(A1) Administrative methods and systems are not adapted to increasing size
	(A2) The company finds itself operating on two markets with completely different problems and opportunities
	(A3) Policy changes applied too superficially; they do not really work their way down to operational level
	(A4) Unsuccessful feelers are not discontinued; they become a financial burden
(B) which required changes in the power system	(B1) Certain key persons lack sufficient time for personal development; they cannot cope with new and more difficult problems
	(B2) Environmental changes threatening the existing power structure are not perceived or acknowledged
	(B3) One branch of operations grows much more rapidly than others; it requires all the company's resources for its development
	(B4) A feeler is 'too' successful for the financial resources and must be disposed of to a company with more capital

Secondly, it also seems from our material that changes concerning the company's external relations more often require a rupture in the power structure. Changes in internal conditions are less likely to lead to any radical change in the existing power system. Thus, in Inmec, it was possible to engage a large number of company members in the organizational analysis which resulted in a transition from a divisionalized to a conglomerate type of organization. But other changes, which among other things involved the discontinuation of a whole branch of operations, disturbed the people most closely concerned—including management—so deeply that the board (and even the dominating stockholder group) had to step in and use their power to enforce the change.

Another rather similar way of classifying structural conflicts has been put forward by Normann (1972). Normann's suggestion is based on his experience as a consultant working with the managements of client companies on historical analyses of their companies' development. This often provided interesting insights into the structural conflicts troubling the companies, but it also offered a fresh explanation of the origins of the conflicts and of management's inability to solve the problem without help. In Normann's view, behind the concrete conflicts between company and environment, or between subsystems in a company, there lies a deeper lack of consonance between management's frame of reference and what the situation actually requires. This is because 'lags' often arise between changes in markets, technology, etc., on the one hand, and the ideas and values applied by management in interpreting and handling their leadership problem on the other. Normann, who has made a special study of product development in companies, suggests that a usual lag of this kind, and one which explains many structural conflicts in companies, is represented by management's attempts to handle innovation problems with a frame of reference developed to deal with a different problem, namely that of keeping a company in balance and counteracting disturbance and variations.

This is an interesting hypothesis. The question still remains, however, of why the lag arose. Is it a result of inadequate management training and of too narrow a professional experience? Or of the fact that radical changes in the idea of leadership in a company often have political consequences? Or of internal emotional blockages in the leaders themselves? Our experience to date suggests that all these explanations are possible. But our material is too slight to justify any conclusions.

Can the Consultant Effect a Change?

If we are to discuss the consultant's chances of effecting a change, we must introduce a set of concepts for describing the interplay between consultant and organization. Our approach is still system-oriented: the consultant is a component or subsystem which, for a time, is included or integrated in the client organization. As before we can start by examining ways in which different subsystems are influenced, after which we can consider the interplay between them. The cognitive system, the power system and the value system are usually those most significantly affected by the consultant or consultant system.

The Consultant and the Cognitive System. The consultant's influence on the cognitive or administrative system is usually the most obvious in the consultant–client relationship. From the literature I cannot think of a single major example of a consultant not trying to influence the cognitive system. In this context there appear to be three main roles that the consultant can play:

1. The role of expert; he introduces information into the organization (technical training, his own previous experience, access to archives, etc.)
2. The role of investigator; he collects, compiles and analyses information.
3. The role of interaction agent; he tries to encourage and improve the exchange of information in the organization.

In fact the roles of expert and investigator are probably often combined, as for instance when Likert and his colleagues help to promote organizational change (see, e.g. Marrow, Bowers and Seashore, 1967). The consultant collects information from some or all employees. In this way he discovers something of the way the organization functions and, in particular about employee morale and various internal relationships. When he feeds this information back to the organization members, he can add a certain amount of expertise: general experience of the functioning of organizations and, perhaps, comparative data from other similar though anonymous organizations.

Management consultants, sociologists, and psychologists who have undertaken such investigations have usually concentrated on internal conditions in the company. Likert, and colleagues of his such as Floyd Mann, have already been mentioned. Argyris (1965) is another well-known example, although in his case the feedback information consists entirely of 'primary' observations (tape recordings of meetings, etc.) Blake and Mouton (1968) can also perhaps be classified as investigators, although part of their method is to let the organization collect much of the information itself. Among market research consultants there is another quite different tradition which involves collecting information about the organization's environment (e.g. what the clients feel about the organization). Among management consultants, however, this is very rare.

The borderline between the investigator role and the interaction agent role is not of course clear-cut. In its pure form the latter means that the consultant brings senders and receivers of information into direct contact with each other, perhaps by arranging meetings and group work and bringing together representatives of various subsystems. Jaques (1951) is a classical example of this type, but most social psychologists describe their efforts to function as change agents in such terms. Ferguson (1966), Bennis (1966) and Hutte (1968) are typical examples.

The Consultant and the Political Defence System. That the consultant wields power, that he must in fact do so if he is to function at all, is rarely acknowledged in discussion of the consultant-client relationship. On the contrary social psychologists in particular frequently emphasize the absence of power as a characteristic of their role and an essential prerequisite of their proper functioning (Shepard, 1965). Thus there is seldom any mention of a consultant's influence on the political system or his relations with the formal power system. Possible exceptions are Jaques (1951) and Whyte and Hamilton (1964). Both these writers admit to having found themselves involved in political processes in the course of consultancy work.

There appear to be two explanations of this taboo. To begin with, the presence of political systems in organizations is seldom if ever openly admitted. Consciously or unconsciously the consultant is affected by this taboo. His ideal, rarely achieved, is never to involve himself in the political game. For other reasons the only legitimate and publicly acknowledged power system—the value-supportive hierarchy—is difficult to discuss. That the consultant's presence in the organization depends on an assignment granted by the management is obvious; the importance of managerial support is often mentioned. Some consultants appear to seek acknowledgement from other power centres as well, perhaps the trade union, the joint industrial council or similar body (cf. Emery, Thorsrund and Lange, 1964). But in view of certain alleged 'rules' of consultancy, relations with the power centres should be kept to a minimum. One of these (which is universally followed) is that personal information is collected from organization members on the condition that it will not be passed on direct to a superior, or in any other way used against the interests of the informant.

But many researchers, perhaps particularly social psychologists, find something alien in the power hierarchy of the organization for deeper reasons than this. They experience it as an evil, an obstacle to organizational self realization. To them a major task is to put the power system at least temporarily out of action.

> It will become even clearer as we examine the strategy implications and instrumentation of the organic model that the main mechanisms for change are (a) redistribution of power based on trust and confidence, leading to functional leadership and (b) conflict resolution based on problem-solving activities, rather than suppression or conflict. These are radical changes; they do away with many of the elements that define bureaucracy, such as status, compartmentalized or individual duties, external control, programmed activities, and so on.

The organic model proposes to realize these changes mainly through a reconstruction of the cognitive maps of individuals. (Bennis, 1963, p. 148)

Naturally a consultant holding such views, which are sharply emotive, will not willingly admit that he has been compelled to engage in the political processes of an organization. Nevertheless it seems to us that the appointment of a consultant, the establishment and development of his assignment, the financial recompense made, and the conclusion of the job, are all part of a total transaction in which the consultant, to function at all, must knowingly strive for some sort of power vis-à-vis the client. The following are some characteristic features of the political process between consultant and client.

A consultant is engaged by a company because some party wishes to effect a change. Or, sometimes, he may be called in because one party wishes to *prevent* a change desired by some other party. Behind the desire to affect a change is an awareness of some sort of problem. The problem occurs within the sphere of interest of the person initiating the assignment. That is to say, either his personal interests or his organizational area of responsibility is affected. The initiator will have certain expectations about the partial or total solution of the problems he has perceived. These expectations provide the motivation for calling in the consultant.

When the consultant accepts the assignment and is introduced into the organization, some person or persons there will formally or informally assume the role of principal, taking over responsibility for the assignment from the initiator. Quite often of course initiator and principal are the same person. From this stage we must also consider as part of the motivation of the assignment the expectations of the principal concerning the solution of the problem as he sees it. In so far as the initiator and the principal are not the same person or group, relations between the two will effect the consultant's standing. The motivations of the initiator and the principal together constitute the *grounds for the assignment*. Because of differences in values and knowledge between client and consultant, in reality the consultant will nearly always work from a broader base than this. This base, which the client *de facto* or following a formal agreement accepts, will here be called the *consultant's action base*.

Every consultant subscribes to certain professional norms which determine what he is prepared to accept as legitimate grounds for an assignment. Quicker results are often required of him with regard to the problems providing the original grounds for the assignment. In negotiating for the action base that he considers necessary, the consultant probably makes use of this fact as a bargaining counter. In the course of his negotiations with the principal an agreement is generally also reached about his economic remuneration. All aspects of the bargaining will then be under continual review as, during the assignment, ideas change on both sides about what the consultant's efforts can accomplish.

Most consultants, and clients for that matter, will tell you that the only workable basis for the transactions between them is mutual trust. In many ways this is certainly true. For instance, the client must be able to rely on the consultant's discretion. But in all reported cases, and in all our case studies, there is in the consultant–client relationship an element of conflict. A game is being played with all the usual trappings: negotiations, opposing strategies, etc. The client likes to 'sound out' the consultant. The client wavers between consultant A and consultant B. He also considers the cost of a particular consultant: will the organization really benefit? Has the consultant perhaps other purposes in mind, beyond his duty to the client? Perhaps he is seeking an opportunity for research or financial reward? The consultant may be particularly anxious to get this assignment. How can he persuade the client to engage him? Or he may be temporarily hard pressed for time. Can he persuade the client to postpone the whole assignment, or some particularly time-consuming part of it? And during the assignment the consultant is often sure to feel that the client is blind to his own best interests, or that he, as consultant, is becoming involved in internal conflicts.

But the game between consultant and client must follow certain strict rules. To some extent every consultant organization has its own norms, but there are also some generally accepted ideas about what would constitute 'manipulation' on the part of a client. Similarly certain ideas about 'decent' client behaviour towards the consultant are generally acknowledged among clients.

The role of the consultant in the cognitive system is closely linked to his role in the political system. For the consultant, as for others, greater access to information confers power. Thus a consultant working partly or entirely as an investigator accumulates power as a project proceeds. Once he has submitted his report, he is suddenly far less powerful.

We have already intimated that political groups may well try to use the engagement of the consultant for their own ends. Other groups may suspect and oppose the engagement on similar grounds; a long and heated struggle can easily develop. The consultant may be aware of what has been going on, or he may realize it only when he discovers that his engagement is tied to certain definite conditions. As we have mentioned earlier, the power of a president is often sharply curtailed by the political system, which means that even an assignment initiated from the top will not necessarily protect the consultant from political intrigue.

But the political system is not simply part of the background. Soon, whether he realizes it or not, the consultant will become a pawn in the political game; his presence will always have some effect on the balance of power, sometimes perhaps a good deal. If he is not politically aware, various interest groups will almost certainly try to use him for their own purposes.

It is not always easy for a consultant to remain politically neutral, even if that is his intention. The most determinedly neutral consultant may find himself acting as a kind of guarantor of peace for the politically weaker elements.

International Meat Packers comprised two independent profit units. On the manufacturing side there was little to distinguish them, but they covered different geographical markets. The larger division was, for the time being, much more profitable; it had great difficulty in satisfying the demands of its market. The smaller unit had been profitable too, but it was now (whether temporarily or permanently was a debatable point) declining both economically and market-wise. For almost a year a consultant worked on a long-range plan together with the president, the administrative director and both the divisional heads. He soon discovered between the two divisional heads a rivalry so deep as to preclude the possibility of any joint use of resources in the present situation. There could be no hope, for instance, that resources freed from the smaller unit could be used to solve the capacity problem of the larger one. The consultant was anxious not to get involved in the political game; he simply tried to make the management group aware of the nature of the problem and to encourage open discussion. Results were surprisingly good. Unanimous agreement was reached: there was to be a radical reorganization along product lines and the old geographical division of the market was to be dropped. A major gain was that able men from the smaller unit could now be better utilized. The head of the smaller division, for instance, was put in charge of all production. Two weeks after this decision had been reached the consultant left the organization. Two weeks later the decision was revoked. The old organization was reinstated almost unchanged. All sorts of explanations were offered. But, after interviews with the people involved, we concluded that, by his very presence and despite all his efforts to remain impartial, the consultant had acted as a kind of umbrella for the weaker unit. After this, things were gradually reorganized. The smaller unit was virtually destroyed; its staff was absorbed into the victorious division in subordinate positions.

The Consultant and the Value System. It has often been pointed out, justifiably, that the idea of the 'value-free' researcher is an illusion. The 'value-free' consultant is possibly an even more unlikely figure. His very willingness to help an organization with its problems is an expression of certain values. For example he presumably believes that 'organizations are useful' and 'organizations should be efficient'. Even if the consultant is unaware of his values, or diffident in expressing them, it will generally be assumed by other people that he represents some values rather than others. Is it therefore possible to classify consultants according to the type of value that they represent and which, by their presence, they will introduce into the organization?

Consultants use very different terms to express their values. Jaques (1951) admits that his aim is the mental health of the organization. Argyris (1965) would like to see organizations based on openness and trust. Bennis (1966) is particularly anxious to equalize power.

But are not all these values in fact closely related? They are anyway all concerned with conditions inside the organization (desirable relations between organization members).

But, as we have previously noted, organizations often have strongly held beliefs about relations with the environment and about the environment itself. The consultant, whether he knows it or not, may also represent values of this sort. In fact many consultants probably regard some such values as a necessary part of their professional responsibility. For instance, companies should obey the laws of society; management is responsible not only to the owners but to society as a whole; certain types of managerial reward are not permissible. Yet other values may be entertained by the consultant as a private person or as an experienced member of his profession. For example, big business is a good thing; internationalization is more important than protectionism; liberal political ideologies are to be favoured. Above all, if the consultant is a trained and practising economist, he is likely, consciously or unconsciously, to support various articles of faith, perhaps that 'nothing must interfere with the market economy'. A lengthy assignment together with a government agency provided us with an interesting example of this: our economic values, geared to adaptability and efficiency, did not always agree with the importance allotted by government employees to the law and legal security.

A technique can be highly infused with values in that its application means a certain priority-setting. For example, a decision at the Registration Office to introduce rationalization budgeting implied an acknowledgment of economic values, and perhaps even an overruling of prevailing law. Efficiency was being weighed against legal security. Whyte (1952) and Stymne (1966) have shown that modern production techniques and electronic data processing can be used to break down professional values that threaten to block an increase in efficiency. I would like to suggest a hypothesis here: one of the major effects of the survey approach of Likert and his colleagues is the possibility of asserting certain values in inter-personal relations. In the same way market surveys favour the affirmation of consumer interests. Values must be operational if they are to be affirmed with any force. In other words if we want to know how far a particular vaiue is being fulfilled, we must have a means of measurement. This is just what the survey techniques supply.

Three Common Consultant Roles

We have seen that a consultant can cooperate with his client organization in various ways; he can also direct his energies in particular to one or other of the various subsystems. It should be possible to classify consultant roles accordingly, bearing in mind the following factors.

(a) What level in the system is the consultant concerned with? Does he try to influence individuals (e.g. the president), groups, departments, divisions, the whole organization?

(b) Does he try to change the production system by direct action?

(c) What role does he play in the cognitive system (information and decision system)? Is he expert, investigator, interaction agent, or a combination of any of these?

(d) Does he seek power? How much? How far does he use it to change the formal power system or the informal political system?

(e) What are his own values? Does he try to alter the company's value system? If so, how much and in what direction?

(f) Does he work alone or in a team of consultants and researchers?

Obviously many roles are theoretically possible. However, the varied literature quoted above, and the experience of consultants and researchers with whom my colleagues and I have discussed these questions, suggests three common types.

The Therapeutic Consultant. The therapeutic consultant has given various names to his approach: the indirect method, the insight method, the power equalization method, etc. In the most typical form of this approach the consultant, who is often a psychologist, a social psychologist, or a psychiatrist, works mainly together with a group or groups—perhaps, for instance, top management. He acts as interaction agent only. The information that he collects through interviews and in other ways, is used only in his own analyses. Any information that is fed back to the group remains in its original form; the group must draw its own conclusions. The consultant is anxious to reduce his own power; as far as possible he avoids involving himself in changes in the power relations. He is simply trying to promote a free and open exchange of information with the group.

For this an obvious lack of interest in the power game and, in general, strict impartiality on his part are essential. He soft-pedals his own evaluations. In other words we can say that he accepts the values upheld by the group and is willing to seek an improvement of the existing organization without essentially upsetting the present power and value systems. The therapeutic consultant usually works alone.

The Power-coopting Consultant. Another type of consultant aligns himself intentionally with a centre of power, such as the board or a major owner interest. He then combines this position with his general expert knowledge and the material collected for the particular assignment. Thus together with an executive centre or on his own, he can suggest and effect changes in all parts of the formal organization. In this way the cognitive system can soon be altered radically: elderly directors can be replaced by younger men with better education, new experts can be engaged, etc., and even the power system beneath the power centre where the consultant temporarily sits can often be radically altered by promotions, loss of power, shifts in power between functions, etc.

The power-coopting consultant is often an organization expert. He may work together with specialist colleagues experienced in particular problems (e.g. market or production). If the company is too small to employ experts in all sections, the consultant will be willing to provide expert knowledge as a supplementary service. He identifies himself wholly with the success of the organization and with economic values such as 'maximum yield on invested capital'. He may try to make board members more aware of economic values. Such values will be effectively supported by the experts he helps to install.

The Supporting Consultant. The supporting consultant combines some of the features of the two types described above, plus some characteristics of his own. He often works at departmental or functional level. He chooses a suitable combination of the expert and interaction agent roles, depending on his evaluations of the competence of the relevant group. He often represents professional values-and norms such as 'know your customer', 'administrative system analysis is more important than the automation of data processing', 'the wage system must leave control of production with management', etc. His influence is based chiefly on professional knowledge which he is prepared to use. Most supporting consultants belong to large consultant firms; when necessary they seek help from colleagues. In this way an assignment may be transferred from one consultant to another within the same firm.

Types of Consultant and Types of Organization
Both moral and practical objections can be raised against all three types of consultant. Some therapists see themselves as a 'superior' brand of

consultant; they apparently fail to realize how easily they can become the tools of management or other power groups. How often can they really effect any major change? All too frequently they get caught up in questions of little importance. The power-coopting consultant is open to the same criticism as any other person who assumes the authority to prescribe change on grounds of superior knowledge and power. Among other things the presence of the supporting consultant may inhibit the awakening of the client's own insight into the relevant problems.

But none of these objections can entirely explain a sharp sense of dissatisfaction with the theory and practice of consultancy. In helping what I have here called corporations, all three types (or a suitable combination) could probably do a passable job. Because the corporation has clear-cut internal goals (profit, growth, etc.), the fact that the therapeutic consultant wants to stabilize the present power and value systems, or that the power-coopting consultant is guided by the demands and expectations of top management, is unlikely to cause any severe damage. On the other hand in the course of our case studies we became increasingly aware that the marginal organization, the appendix organization, and the institution often have nothing better to hope for than the help of the supporting consultant.

For small companies and other marginal organizations the cost of the professional advice of the supporting consultant is often high; it may also herald a premature development towards corporation status. None of the types of consultant described can do much in the way of developing and supporting external goals in the appendix organization or the institution.

Our research on the subject is not yet ready for publication, but I can indicate briefly the way in which we have approached the problem.

Consulting in Marginal Organizations. The most valuable asset of the successful small company is its quickness in sensing changes in the environment and making the necessary adjustments. The demands that this makes on the cognitive system were discussed in Chapter 5.

One of the greatest risks of consulting in the marginal organization is that the client becomes overdependent on the consultant. The consultant may be given a permanent position in the organization, responsible perhaps for financial planning or economic evaluations. Naturally some such arrangement may be very convenient as part-time employment. But it is not consulting work as I mean it here. Rather should the consultant try to encourage in the client an awareness of the special demands that are made on the non-dominating company; the client should be helped to accept the need for change and to extend the range of his contacts.

Too much success can land the marginal organization in serious difficulties. Lacking the resources to utilize the success to the full, it either has to face competition from invaders or attach itself to a corporation which possesses resources big enough to dominate the new territory. Lack of resources imposes another problem on the marginal company: risky experiments are too expensive; everything the company undertakes must succeed.

These are only some of the difficulties which affect the consultant's position in the marginal organization. Because of them, it will probably be necessary for the consultant to establish a special relationship with the leader of the organization. He must help the leader to develop his own possibilities; at the same time he cannot assume the neutral role of the therapist. He will probably have to act as an expert; if possible he should be able to teach various techniques adapted to the needs of the small company, such as market investigation and market experimentation. The consultant must bear in mind that marginal organizations often grow into appendix organizations or corporations; nevertheless he must not automatically try to transform every marginal organization into a corporation. He should not, for instance, always encourage small companies, regardless of their status, to invest more in product development and marketing.

Consulting in Appendix Organizations. The commonest problem of the appendix organization is the unsatisfactory nature of its relations with the principal. The power to formulate goals, and the responsibility, lies with the parent company or, in the case of government agencies, with a central department. But the body which possesses information about the environment and about the opportunities open to the appendix organization is the organization itself. Once or twice, in such situations, we tried to help the managements of appendix organizations to formulate goals and long-range plans themselves. This implies a step towards institution or corporation status. Sometimes of course this may be beneficial to all parties. But we became increasingly aware that it is more often a poor substitute for a real dialogue between the principal and the appendix organization about the best way of jointly achieving the principal's goals. This represents a major field for innovation: to find forms for such cooperation, or any sort of better contact, between parent and appendix organization. Many large international concerns as well as national government agencies would stand to gain from this.[20]

Consulting in Institutions. Institutions often have to struggle with very complicated problems. Like the large company they have to develop and adapt systems with a view to dominating the environment and extending their territory; they also have to formulate external goals. Many co-operatives find it difficult at the present time to adapt their external goals to the real needs of the environment in a way that their members can accept as meaningful. The commonest solution seems to be to let the external goals quietly fade away, possibly to be replaced by quasi-goals such as 'promote competition', 'maintain quality', etc. Consultants often actively encourage the transformation from institution into corporation;

for instance they may introduce experts and administrative techniques that promote purely economic values and other internal goals such as growth.

Suppose, then, that the management of an institution is trying to steer the organization towards corporation status. New external goals that are meaningful, practicable and attractive must be found. But this alone is not enough. Management must have the power to effect the necessary changes in the value-supportive system. The power systems of institutions are often very complex; it is not at all easy to change them. The consultant must help to make management aware of the difficulties. He must also, presumably, be able to suggest ways of finding external goals that are important, challenging, and fitted to the resources and history of the institution. But there must be no question of the consultant assuming the institutional leadership: he must make no direct suggestions nor assert any specific external goals. This would only serve to reduce management's own ability to transform the institution.

Appendix 1

Some Basic Differences Between Biological and Organized Systems

Organizations Are Not Born and Do Not Die

Although the expression 'the birth of an organization' has sometimes been used (e.g. Simon, 1953), it must be emphasized that organizations are not born in the biological sense. Even when a new organization arises through the severance of a department from a parent organization, the expression is still extremely misleading. Character traits cannot be inherited by a new organization in the sense that a biological individual can inherit characteristics from earlier generations. Admittedly, experiences as a department in the parent company can affect the development of the new organization; so can any experience gleaned by its founders (the original organization members) elsewhere. We have seen illustrations of this in several of the companies that we have studied. One building and construction firm, for example, had been founded by a small group of engineers who broke away from an older company (a common procedure in that particular industry); it was then natural for them to build on their common organizational experiences—even if this partly took the form of a reaction against old ways. They had all learned, for instance, how not to behave towards customers. But the decisive factor that moulded the new firm during the first ten years or so was the first big assignment.

Perhaps the most dramatic difference between living and organized systems is that the individual organism has a limited life-span, whereas we can say that organizations, both theoretically and in practice, can enjoy eternal life.

In terms of systems theory, death can be defined as a rapid disintegration of the individual's structure. We know that this process is irreversible. Once disintegration has set in, the individual cannot be resurrected. The study of organizations has revealed no equivalent process. Two organizations that merge tend to retain the major part of their original structures; a comparatively small organization taken over by a larger one retains a substantial part of its structure; even when an organization is formally

172

discontinued, some parts of it—some departments for example—may remain active in another organization.

Organizations that appear to have been destroyed irrevocably, can suddenly revive (the German economy after World War II provided several examples of this). And perhaps most important of all: we know of no processes that are essential to the maintenance of organizational life— processes whose cessation would inevitably lead to the death of the organization. On the contrary, there is a tendency towards eternal life. To destroy an organization requires an enormous conscious effort, which is often unsuccessful. (Typical examples: attempts to wipe out guerilla operations or an undesirable political movement.)

We all know the explanation but often forget to take it into account. The network of relations operating in the organization is retained, wholly or in part, in each of the organization members; all that is needed is for one or more of these persons to decide to revive the organization. Cells and parts of the body (fortunately?) lack this ability. The organization, or a part of it, can continue to live in a new guise (possibly as part of a larger organization).

No Life Cycle

Another factor, closely related to the differences we have just been discussing, is that the biological individual has a definite life cycle, which organizations presumably lack. Selznick (1957), Zetterberg (1962), Blake (Blake *et al.*, 1966) and others have suggested that there is a certain regular pattern in the historical development of organizations. Selznick suggests that a new organization first seeks recognition from a hostile environment and tries to create for itself a distinctive competence. As this develops, the organization grows, and in the process becomes more bureaucratically organized. Blake and his colleagues have recognized similar processes. They speak of three phases in developing companies: the entrepreneurial stage, the mechanistic stage and, lastly, the dynamic stage. Zetterberg suggests instead that the organization develops in cycles geared mainly to the replacement of a particular type of leader by another complementary type, as required for the growth of the organization.

These observations have been confirmed by our case studies, in that we generally found it necessary to look carefully into the history of a company before we could even begin to understand its present structure. Examples of our historical analyses have been published separately (Hellgren *et al.*, 1968, and Sandkull and Stymne, 1968). It can be seen that organizational growth does sometimes reveal interesting features, many of which recur again and again. The literature is full of examples: growth leads to a bureaucratic organization; a decentralization phase is likely to be followed by some resumption of centralized control; a crisis is often followed by a

new period of prosperity, etc. However, none of these phases have anything to do with life cycles of Selznick's type, nor with recurrent cycles of
the kind forseen by Zetterberg. They are essentially the product of environmental factors. There are, for example, periods of expansion, crises in the
industry, wars, major successes or failures; or perhaps cooperation is
established with another organization, part of whose policy may be
'catching'; a new president may be appointed; a liquidity crisis may follow
the imposition of credit restrictions. The increasingly complex structure of
an organization that is growing in both size and experiences is not determined by any inherited traits, nor does it undergo any predictable phases
or cycles. Instead, the morphogenesis of an organization (to borrow the
biologists' term for the ability of a biological system to acquire an increasingly complex structure) seems to have something of the character
of a learning process which, to a very great extent, can be consciously
influenced.[21] We shall see later that for a certain type of organization the
planning of this learning process does more than anything else to promote
adjustment to a changing environment.

The Concrete Organism and the Abstract Organization

In two essays on living systems Miller (1965a, b and c) distinguishes
between three types of system: the concrete, the abstracted, and the con-
ceptual. He then proceeds to discuss living systems, seeing them in the
main as concrete. One of the chief distinctions between organisms and
organizations can be expressed in terms of this classification. Organisms
are, in the main, concrete systems; organizations can, in the main, be
described as abstracted or abstract systems.

Of course, we could say that a steelworks can be usefully described as
a concrete system of machines, material flows, etc. But we can hardly hope
to explain the type of organizational problem with which we are now con-
concerned, i.e. innovativeness, the dysfunctions of bureaucratic organization, individual adaptiveness and motivation, interperson and intergroup
conflict, etc—in any other than highly abstract terms. Some of the basic
concepts which would have to be considered are: information channels,
programming, environmental awareness, power, status, role expectations.
And this is not just because organizational sociology has a weakness for
abstract descriptions; at least in part it is because life in organizations is
essentially abstract and symbolical. Thus, various situations are possible
which would be remarkable, to say the least, if we were regarding the
organization as a biological system: a company president can be physically
absent for a long period but still exert considerable influence on the
organization by means of his symbolical presence; the status system may be
invisible to all except the members of the organization; the efficiency can
never be measured in terms of horse-power, operational effectiveness, etc.

Dependence on Individual Component Parts and on Environment

Living and organized systems differ radically in another important respect. Most organisms, particularly the higher organisms (e.g. man), are complete, i.e. they can exist independently of other organisms. But whereas parasitism and symbiosis are the exception among biological individuals, among organizations they are the rule. Few, if any, organizations are constructed like organizational Robinson Crusoes. We have only to think of the problems of trying to establish a power station or a mine, perhaps, in an isolated area, to understand the difficulties. Contrariwise, living organisms are generally completely dependent on at least some of their component parts, whereas organizations seem able to lose components and still survive in a modified form. We have of course recently become accustomed to the idea of heart transplants for both animals and men, but these are essentially artificial operations. They do not reflect any natural characteristic of the organism. In organizations similar losses are quite possible: a production department may be closed down (in which case the company probably adapts by transferring its activities elsewhere); an accounts department may be out of action for a long time while computers are being introduced; a company president may be away sick for long periods at a time. Some kind of adjustment is always possible. Practical examples of this phenomenon have been well documented in the past and need hardly be added to here. However, one example from our material seems worth relating.

> Because an organization can survive the temporary or even permanent loss of seemingly 'vital' parts, it is possible among other things to introduce radical programmes for savings or rationalization. Let us take the example of personnel. Organization members often have the idea that 'you can't reduce personnel below a certain minimum'. However, one of our case studies shows that almost anything is possible when it comes to 'banting'. Between 1950 and 1965 the Brickman Company had grown into a successful medium-sized building firm, operating in several parts of the country and employing about 200 clerical workers and 800 building operatives. However, as a result of several heavy losses, the firm became insolvent. The official receiver was nevertheless anxious for the firm to continue and imposed a drastic reduction in clerical workers, from 200 to 50. Annual turnover also fell, but only by an acceptable amount from about 300 to 200 million crowns a year. The new president felt that the smaller organization functioned in many ways better than the old one.

Perhaps the most remarkable feature of the organized system is that several subsystems can be combined in almost any number of ways. In the public administration particularly, it is quite common for organizations to be dismembered and recombined, sometimes in a way that seems almost haphazard. Naturally, such operations are not without complications, but nobody expects the organizations to die or even to sicken in any biological sense.

Disintegration of Organization Structures—A Note on Vincent Peele, Matthew Cooley and Alfred Marrow

Background

Few detailed studies have been made of actual change processes, and even fewer with the focus on top management. The rare accounts that do exist are therefore all the more interesting. I have chosen three examples, in each of which a new man has just arrived as head of a company. A study of the subsequent events provides a rewarding complement to the material presented in this report.

Gouldner describes the advent of Vincent Peele as local manager of a gypsum plant. Peele found an established 'indulgency pattern', which he tried to shatter (Gouldner, 1954). Guest (1962) analyses the case of Matthew Cooley. Cooley was appointed manager of an automobile assembly plant whose internal weaknesses were causing top management to consider its closure. Within two and a half years, under Cooley's management, it had become one of the best units in the company. Alfred Marrow tells us how he took over a pyjama factory and managed to reverse a downward trend (Marrow, Bowers and Seashore, 1967).

Below is a brief description of the main features in the three change processes. I conclude with a few comments on my own interpretation, which differs essentially from that of the writers concerned.

Vincent Peele

Vincent Peele was appointed local manager of the Oscar Centre branch of the General Gypsum Company in 1948. The previous manager, an elderly man, had recently died. The plant had 225 employees, 75 working in the mine and 150 in various surface departments. The most important of these was the 'board plant'.

Before Peele took over he was thoroughly briefed by head office. He was told of his predecessor's weaknesses, which seemed to consist mainly of a general tendency to let things slip through overindulgence. Peele was not only to tighten things up: he was to improve production to the level required by the pressures of post-war competition. As Gouldner puts it, Peele 'came to the plant sensitized to the rational and impersonal yard-sticks which his superiors would use to judge his performance' (Gouldner, 1954, p. 71).

He started by replacing some of the key personalities of the old régime, among them the personnel manager. He also introduced various bureau-cratic rules and innovations which were strictly enforced. This was some-thing entirely new in a plant that had always prided itself on being one big happy family.

A typical—and typically unpopular—disciplinary measure was the intro-duction of 'warning notices' containing a list of possible offences, such as drinking or gambling at work, lateness, absence, disobedience, etc. An offender would receive a notice complete with details of his particular offence, which he and his immediate superiors had to sign in acknowledge-ment of the warning.

It is not very surprising that this, and the whole apparently harsh system that it represented, was deeply resented by the workers. Their earlier positive feelings for their company drained away, and much energy went into finding ways of getting round the hated new regulations.

Nevertheless the huge effort to raise production and reduce waste, accidents and production costs, probably gave some results. But, as Gouldner points out, there was no method for measuring or evaluating the effects of the increase in bureaucracy.

Matthew Cooley

Cooley started from almost diametrically opposite premises. His approach was also in sharp contrast to Peele's. The assembly plant—plant Y—of which he became manager in 1953 employed between two and five thousand workers, depending on the level of production. Cooley's predecessor had been dismissed for failure to improve production and quality.

Under the old régime pressure from headquarters had been kept up almost continuously: divisional specialists, dealing with accounting, per-sonnel, quality control and most other functions, visited plant Y far more often than any of the other plants. At the same time pressure made itself felt from customers who lodged frequent complaints about late deliveries and defective work. Relations between the local manager and his staff were suffering as a result. The local people felt, probably with some justification, that their manager tried to put the blame for the plant's failures on them.

Now, by changing the local manager, central headquarters intended to abandon the old system of detailed directives and strict controls and to try out a completely new way of running the plant. The new manager, Cooley, was given a free rein. He saw it as one of his main tasks to protect the plant from interference from headquarters. To everyone's surprise, not least that of the local department heads, he fired none of his immediate colleagues. Instead he listened, made himself familiar with the technical problems, set up committees and, in consultation with his colleagues, introduced several technical improvements. But even before this he set out to improve general working conditions. He cleared up the old cafeteria, the toilets and the changing-rooms, introducing better ventilation and air conditioning. Next he tackled storage facilities and conveyors, loading and unloading routines, and production lines. Everywhere he tried to improve the physical work flow, reducing bottlenecks and other dislocations.

It took some time to make the changes and it was a year or two before results began to show. But two and a half years later the plant had achieved a leading position in the division, judged on productivity, quality and other yardsticks. Cooley was promoted elsewhere but the favourable trend continued.

Alfred Marrow

In 1962 the Harwood Manufacturing Corporation took over its main competitor, the Weldon Manufacturing Company. The result was a merger between two companies of roughly the same size, each employing about 1,000 people, and both engaged in the manufacture and sales of the same product: pyjamas. But while Harwood was geared to low-cost production, selling mostly to department store chains, Weldon manufactured quality products which it sold to specialist stores under its own brand name. The reason for Harwood's action was financial: the company had underutilized capital. It was intended originally that the two companies should continue to operate independently and that Weldon should retain its own organization. But it soon became obvious that Weldon, which had previously been run almost entirely by two partner-owners, was suffering from serious internal weaknesses.

Instead of coordination, there was jealousy and suspicion between its merchandizing organization, located in New York under one partner, and the manufacturing people in Philadelphia who were responsible to the other partner. One source of misunderstanding was that many administrators were located in Philadelphia because costs were lower there, but these officials were often regarded by the manufacturing people as spies for the New York management.

The manufacturing division in particular revealed numerous inefficiencies, with an imbalance between its control and recordkeeping side, which had too many members and a considerable duplication of records, and its management side which had too little staff. One industrial engineer with one assistant, for instance was expected to deal entirely with rate study and machine layout. There was no electronic data processing, although economically this would have been possible, no research and development programme and no personnel department.

Manufacturing and merchandizing functioned as independent, uncoordinated units. The lack of understanding and communication between them led in turn to further conflicts. Manufacturing took little account of the pressure from customers to which the salesmen were exposed. The salesmen, who were generally paid on a commission basis, would make optimistic and sometimes mutually conflicting promises to customers about styles or delivery times, without allowing for the considerable cost and inconvenience to the manufacturing side of frequent changes in production priorities.

All this meant that the Weldon organization could not be retained in its present form. Something radical clearly had to be done. Alfred Marrow, president of Harwood and a doctor of social psychology, decided to call in a team of behavioural scientists to educate Weldon's management and improve its morale, and two groups of engineering consultants to make technological changes. At the same time he invited the Survey Research Centre at Michigan University to observe the change process and to record, measure and assess events as they took place.

A whole series of countermeasures was introduced. The assortment was reduced, planning was streamlined and, following some changes in the organization and improvements in the reporting system, decision making was decentralized. Coordination and consultation between interdependent departments was strengthened, at the same time as changes in plant layout tended to reduce many interdependencies. Technical equipment was brought up to date, and improvements in training and personnel policy led to greater job satisfaction and a lower labour turnover. The list of measures is long and contains on the whole what one would expect.

Results were satisfactory. Costs fell; efficiency and employee attitudes improved. No radical personnel changes were necessary. When the original difficulties had been overcome, it became clear that the organization possessed large but hitherto latent resources. Almost all its members were prepared to lend their active cooperation.

Some Comments

In all three studies the descriptions are thorough and the analyses penetrating. Nevertheless the main argument, which is more or less the same in them all, seems to me incomplete and misleading.

Gouldner is really trying ot expose the negative consequences of Peele's bureaucratic approach. In paritcular he probes the real reasons for the increase in bureaucracy, which he feels cannot be entirely explained by the need to improve efficiency.

In any event, emphasis will be placed upon the role of factors, other than those required for technical efficiency, that increase the degree of bureaucratization. (Gouldner, 1954, p. 26)

He concludes that management could have chosen to tackle the problem differently.

Concretely, this study suggests that there is a choice that may be made, a choice between two *possible* alternatives, between punishment-centered and representative bureaucratization. (Gouldner, 1954, p. 26)

Guest's main line of thought is the same, and he can cite the greater success of Matthew Cooley in support of his thesis. Marrow makes the same diagnosis, in fact he admits that he made it at a very early stage when he recognized that the chief cause of the difference in performance between the two very similar companies lay in their opposite leadership styles. Harwood encouraged participation in discussing and dealing with problems, while Weldon was run according to the traditional authority-oriented pattern.

Once the basic difference in approach to management of the organizations was recognized, the task became one of introducing organizational changes into the Weldon enterprise that would bring the Harwood management approach into play—and to do so quickly, smoothly, and with the least human and financial cost. (Marrow *et al.*, 1967, pref. XV)

I do not mean to deny that Vincent Peele might have been more successful if he had shared the belief of the other two in participative management. The advantages of this type of leadership—and its limitations—are well known. It corresponds most closely to what the workers expect; it matches prevailing social values and, at least in these three cases, the technological requirements of the situation. On the other hand, to achieve results of the kind needed, a changeover to democratic or participative management was obviously not enough on its own.

Matthew Cooley's main contribution was his own experience and technical competence; Alfred Marrow's was also technical competence, as embodies in the various skilled consultants whom he introduced. Decisive to success in both cases was that outside disturbances and variations (from central office, customers, etc.) was reduced; the aim was to achieve an organization with better internal coordination. In describing the Cooley case, Guest quotes a foreman:

But . . . it began to dawn on us that if we ever were to stop running around and putting out fires, we had to do this. [i.e. get together at meetings and start planning]. *Also, just getting together as a group was worth something in itself.* (Guest, 1962, p. 47)

The italics are Guest's. The idea he has chosen to emphasize by these italics is of course interesting, but in my view the previous sentence is the one that provides the greatest insight into Cooley's methods. Its significance was clearly also felt by others in the company. For example, quoting Guest again:

They [the foremen] were saying, in effect, that greater motivation was not a consequence of more rewarding interpersonal relationships alone; they placed equal stress on the elimination of technical 'bottlenecks' as a rewarding experience in itself. (Guest, 1962, p. 55).

In the terminology of the present report, these three cases illustrate conditions where variations and disturbances have caused structural disintegration in organizations; they also illustrate three more or less successful attempts to repair a disintegrating structure and restore efficiency. In two of them participative management happened to be one of the tools used by the new leaders. However, I feel considerable doubt as to whether this particular tool was necessary to the subsequent success, suitable though it can be in many cases.

Description of Organizations as Systems

The Organization and Its Subsystems

For a researcher describing a system, a major problem is the choice of subsystems and components. Organizational theory is full of suggestions, one or two of which I have already mentioned in Chapter 4. Let us now look at a few more.

Fayol's (1949) classical division into technical, commercial, financial, safety, accounting and administrative activities is one of the commonest classifications. Barnard's (1938) inducements-contribution model represents an entirely different division, mainly because the author emphasizes organizational dependence on environment. My own work (Rhenman, 1964) provides an example of a cybernetic, or control-and-regulation, branch of organization theory. Here the emphasis is on the two main organizational subsystems: the productive system and the system of control (the administrative system).

Parsons (1960) seems to combine all aspects of these three approaches in his model. He suggests that every social system must have subsystems fulfilling four functions, namely adaptation to the environment, goal fulfilment, integration of subsystems, and the maintenance of values. Pfiffner and Sherwood (1960) see the formal organization as the central system, modified by a number of subsystems ('overlays'): the sociometrical contact network, the functional contact system, the network of decision centres, the power situation and the communication channels.

The trend apparent in the last few years can perhaps best be illustrated by Katz and Kahn (1966). These authors are well aware that the structures of organizations are complex and varied and that the problem of identifying subsystems can be approached in many ways. In some degree following Parsons (1960), they postulate five basic subsystems: productive, maintenance, supportive, adaptive and managerial. Among writers who have chosen a classification into subsystems suitable to a particular purpose the best known are perhaps Emery and Trist (1960), who divide the organization into a social and a technical system, and Burns and Stalker (1966), who postulate as the three main subsystems the work system, the status system and the political system.

The division into subsystems is to some extent arbitrary, depending entirely on the purpose of the particular writer. Before I make—and attempt to justify—my own choice, I must introduce a few relevant concepts.

Some Types of Subsystem

It is important to distinguish between two types of system, which depend on the way the system is defined. The two types are: [22]

1. Systems can be defined by their components. Such systems can be subdivided into those consisting of concrete and those consisting of abstract components. A factory comprising a number of machines, clerical staff and operatives, and a computer, is an example of such a subsystem defined in terms of a series of concrete components. Thus, when Emery and Trist (1960) describe an organization as a socio-technical system, they are referring to two concrete subsystems: the system of persons and the system of technical resources. A simple example of a system consisting of abstract components is a role system comprising a foreman's role, a planning engineer's role, and several operative roles. Burns' description of the work system, the political system, the career system, and the values that each of these embodies, represents a rather complex description of subsystems defined in terms of abstract components.

2. Functional systems on the other hand are defined in terms of the function that they fulfil in relation to (i.e. their effect on) environment, other subsystems, etc. Parsons' classification, already referred to, is a typical example.

It is important to note these differences for the following reason. If an organized system is defined by its components (concrete and/or abstract), it is often difficult to pin down its functions (effects), which are likely to be many and varied. If on the other hand a system is defined by its function, it is often difficult to identify its components, some of which may simultaneously belong to other subsystems. In living systems this difficulty does not appear to be so marked (the heart, kidneys, etc. have definite functions).

If we are to be able to describe a functional subsystem at all, we often have to limit ourselves to an incomplete system, i.e. one which fulfils a particular function, as a result of interaction with another (supportive) subsystem. The production system of a company, for example, is often an incomplete subsystem which can only operate through interaction with subcontractors.

Examples of Some Important Subsystems

In the above report my choice of components and subsystems is also, in principle, arbitrary. It, too, is geared solely to my present purpose. But before making the final choice I had naturally already made a number of important decisions which restricted my subsequent freedom of action. For instance I had already chosen my general approach to the description of organizational environments. My specific approach was also affected by the descriptive framework within which I was working. I am an organization theorist and, as such, I expect to be able to make a fruitful analysis from a fairly high systems level. Machines, people and groups are the smallest unit of study; usually the altitude is higher, with components such as groups of machines, departments, etc. These, then, are the restrictions. On this basis I have discussed some concrete systems such as the management group, some abstract systems such as the system of norms and, in particular, some functional systems such as the development system. Wherever necessary these systems have been defined and described in the text. The functional subsystems which in my opinion are particularly important are: the productive system, the administrative (or cognitive) system, the value system, the value-supportive system and the defence system, for which reason the last three of these have been dealt with in the main body of the report.

Two Examples

The Productive System. The productive system can be defined as either a concrete subsystem or a functional subsystem. In the former case it is defined as a system of material-processing components; in the latter as the subsystem that fulfils the productive function. In most industrial companies this is an important function in relation to the environment.

Productive systems can be characterized in many ways. The nature of the material flow determines its character as a batch production system or a continuous production system. The amount of programming determines its character as handicraft or industrialized production. The number of production units determines its character as a unit-, a series-, or a batch-production system. Another major feature of the productive system is the width of the assortment. These various characteristics have been discussed and illustrated in Rhenman (1969). The interdependence of components in the system has also been treated by Thompson (1967). He distinguishes between pooled interdependence, sequential interdependence, and reciprocal interdependence.

Most of these characteristics of productive systems can be described in flow diagrams or matrices showing the components or stages in the material-processing and the intercomponent material flows.

The Administrative System (The Cognitive System). The administrative system, too, can be described as either a concrete or a functional subsystem. In the former case it is defined as the system of information-processing and information-storing components and the designation 'cognitive system' may then be more suitable. In the latter it can be defined, for example, as the subsystem that controls and changes the productive system, thus promoting adaptation to environmental change and uncertainty or counteracting fluctuations and uncertainty generated in other subsystems.

As a concrete system the administrative system can be divided in various ways. For example, we can speak of the budget system, the formal reporting system, etc., indicating subsystems made up of recognizable components. The administrative system can also be divided into functional subsystems such as production control and stakeholder administration, the former controlling production flow and the latter seeking to influence the environment (e.g. personnel administration and marketing). The various subsystems are exemplified in Rhenman (1969). The most complete general model for describing administrative systems is provided by Ramström (1967).

The development system is also part of the administrative system. It, too, can be described as either a system of components or a functional subsystem. Development departments or sets of development projects can be regarded as concrete or abstract component subsystems. Usually, however, development systems seem to be defined as functional subsystems. Their task is to adjust the organization to structural changes in the environment. The rationalization system can be seen mainly as a system for adjusting the organization to changes in the price of production factors or in the available technology, and to some extent for satisfying the demand of the environment for ever greater productivity.

A Note on the Causal Texture of Organizational Environments

Four Types of Environment

Earlier we mentioned Emery and Trist's ambitious attempt to classify organizational environments (Emery and Trist, 1965). Their classification is based on the findings of researchers at the Tavistock Institute who worked, rather like ourselves, as consultants in a variety of organizations. The keystone of their approach is the interconnectedness of environmental components, although certain other environmental features interest them too. The following are the four types of environment suggested by Emery and Trist.

1. The randomized environment. The environmental elements are placid and randomly distributed throughout the environment. There is thus no connection between environmental parts. Knowledge about one element is no help in dealing with any other.
2. The clustered (structured) environment. This type of environment is also placid but the environmental elements are not randomly distributed. Instead they hang together in certain ways, often in different clusters. Knowledge about some elements can, therefore, be of help in dealing with others.
3. The disturbed-reactive environment. This can be described as a structured environment containing competitive elements. Because of the presence of competitors, an organization in such an environment will sometimes experience the environment reacting to its own behaviour. The ability to deal with reactions in the environment (e.g. by avoiding or hindering competitors) becomes an important requisite of survival.
4. The turbulent environment. In this type of environment the elements are dependent on each other in a variety of ways. Changes are generated and reproduce themselves in the environment both dependently and independently of the behaviour of the individual organization.

Organizations in the randomized environment have no need of strategies. All they need is 'the simple tactic of attempting to do one's best on a purely local basis'. In the clustered and reactive environments survival will depend on plans for dealing with the environment. In the turbulent environment the organization cannot expect to survive through its own efforts alone. To deal with this type of environment it is necessary to have overriding value systems and/or overall forms of organization strong enough to counteract the tendency of the environmental elements to destroy each other. These overall organizations are called matrix organizations.

An Example

Emery and Trist further state that the environment of any particular organization may very well develop from the simplest to the most complex of these four types during the lifetime of the organization. The authors describe two examples, one concerning an industrial company and the other a professional association. At an early stage in our case studies we were most attracted by Emery and Trist's approach. We felt that they provided a strikingly apt description of one of 'our' environments, namely the Swedish building and construction industry. Developments in this field resemble in many respects a gradual transition from the simplest to the most complex of the four types described above.

> The tendering of contracts has long been the major environmental element in the building industry. Contracts are environmental elements randomly distributed in time and place. Even their size is a random feature. A great many contractors have been working on this market and tactical skill has been the main requirement for survival. Three skills have been particularly important: to calculate correctly, to get paid for extra work, and to recruit good supervisors for the individual projects.

> However, over the years, this environment has assumed a structure. There are now considerable differences between contracts, for example: road construction, power plant construction, tunnelling, the building of large residential areas, the building of one-family homes, industrial construction, repair work, etc. The market has become clustered round a small number of customers and in certain geographical areas (Stockholm, southern Sweden, and the areas around Gothenburg, Lake Mälar and Sundsvall). Cyclical variations, resulting from the planned use of the industry as an economic regulator, has introduced a time structure into the environment. The organizations involved have developed various strategies for dealing with the new situation. There is a growing interest in product specialization, although usually tempered by the realization that 'putting all your eggs in one basket' can be risky. Companies which happen to have been established in

the 'wrong' markets plan new locations in expanding areas. Stable cooperation with certain clients or types of client (housing associations, local authorities, industrial combines, etc.) is another strategy used, consciously or unconsciously, by the successful companies; also, to counteract economic fluctuations, the acquisition of ground for building under their own auspices is important.

The competitive and reactive elements were of course always present in the environment, but they only became really significant as a structure came to be imposed. In the randomized environment the problem of competition was resolved in one of two ways: either the organization tried to survive by virtue of its superior tactics (skill in calculation, in recruiting good supervisors, etc.) or a manoeuvre known as encirclement was resorted to. Competition was neutralized by means of an agreement with competitors in the relevant field of operations about who should get which projects.

Neither of these solutions will work satisfactorily in the structured environment, where a competitor with a superior strategy can easily outmanoeuvre all the rest. All the leading companies have this as their aim, whether they realize it or not. The others are either vanquished outright or they accept defeat and sell. All this has meant considerable rationalization in the industry during the last few years.

These changes, generated within the industry, affect one another. They are also affected by changes in the world outside. The picture that emerges coincides very well with the description of the turbulent environment. We have mentioned the concentration to a small number of customers. These now begin to make demands; at the same time they open perspectives hitherto unknown in the industry, for instance as they begin to recognize the technical advantages embodied in the wider expertise of the large building corporations.

Thus, the organizations strive to stabilize relations with the customers. At the same time the customers themselves follow strategies in some degree parallel and in some conflicting. On the one hand they desire a stable relationship, to promote the creation of more qualified building companies. At the same time they are afraid of discarding competition altogether.

Recent advances in technology and administration are making

themselves felt in the industry; there is much confused thinking about 'system building' and great controversy about the use of electronic data processing. The consequences of internationalization are often discussed, but nobody really knows what to expect or how to react.

Criticism of Emery and Trist

In many respects I found Emery and Trist's approach thought-provoking and rewarding although, as I explained in Chapter 3, I ultimately chose an essentially different way of describing the organization's environment. In the main, I objected to their classification on three counts.

1. All environments contain some random elements, some clustering, some risk of reaction and a certain amount of structural change. In our case histories it is certainly possible to discern a gradual shift in the relative importance of the different environmental features, but this is hardly the chief characteristic of the environment. Building companies always have to deal somehow with random disconnected environmental changes; they are always likely to encounter unfriendly reactions from the environment and to come up against structural changes; at the same time, as far as possible, such companies try to map internally and to utilize in some way the structure of the environment.
2. The four classes of environment suggested by Emery and Trist leave no room for distinguishing between different types of value environments. For my views on this subject the reader is referred to Chapter 3.
3. Structural changes in the environment need not always be a disadvantage. For organizations that can dominate their environment in particular, such changes can be of positive value. In this context I question Emery and Trist's claim that some sort of matrix organization is needed to deal with the turbulent environment. It seems to me that their conclusion is based on a number of very special cases. We came across a hint of such an idea once: in the industry where the Interior Decorating Company operated, there was some discussion of a government commission or an industrial combine, either of which could have been described as a matrix organization. What will probably happen, however, is that sooner or later some company in the industry will seize the initiative (the Interior Decorating Company has plans in that direction). In future this company will then be able to dominate the environment and steer environmental developments to its own advantage.

Below I summarize the three main ways that I have suggested for describing environments. These ideas have been developed in the main text of the report.

1. I suggest a distinction between reversible changes (variations and stochastic changes) and irreversible changes (structural changes). These changes are often intertwined with one another in the environmental elements, but the mechanisms available to the organizations for dealing with them will be quite different.

2. I suggest a distinction between changes in the task environment and changes in the value environment. The organization's trickiest problems are connected with changes in the value environment.

3. The way in which organizations deal with environmental changes depends essentially on the type of goals that they entertain. I have therefore suggested a classification into marginal organizations, appendix organizations, corporations and institutions.

System Development and Advantages of Scale

An important principle for system development emerges from the discussion in Chapter 5. It is generally advantageous to make the boundaries of a system as wide as possible. In our material the National Rationalization Office provided the most interesting and complex example of the problems involved in defining the limits of a system.

> In considering how to define the limits of its rationalization work, NRO was divided into three camps. One claimed that traditional method studies applied to the commonest office tasks would be the best way of achieving personnel cuts. Another believed in the development and installation of integrated data-processing systems. The third pinned its faith on total studies of the major government agencies.

In conclusion I suggest three postulates. These are no more than hypotheses, but they contain the essence of my argument concerning the advantages of scale resulting from system development. Let us remind ourselves of the three types of resources necessary in combination with system development, namely:
1. a superior system
2. knowledge of the environment, making it possible to select a homogeneous subsystem in the environment and to direct resources towards the further development of this subsystem
3. resources for forcing the superior system on the environment.
   A weakness in one of these resources can to some extent be compensated by extra strength in one of the others. Probably, though, the three factors are interrelated.

Postulate of Least Expected Advantage

Knowledge of the environment $\times$ Relative advantage in the system $>$ M where M is a minimum value

Greater knowledge of the market makes it easier to identify a market segment towards whose conquest resources can be directed. But if the system enjoys some special advantage or advantages, knowledge of the market will not be so vital. In certain industries (e.g. food, banking or the automobile industry) where the threshold of invention to overcome is very high, companies must commit large resources to market studies. In other industries (e.g. electronics or chemicals) where technical innovation is more frequent, market research has always been assigned a much less important position.

Postulate of Size of System and Relative Advantage

Relative advantage of new system $\times$ Size of system $> N$, where N is a minimum value

Naturally the technical and scientific advances in any particular field will to some extent determine the size of the relative advantage that an organization can offer the environment by its new products and systems. However, as we have already seen, the size of the system also does much to determine the relative advantage. This is in fact probably the most important factor except at a very early stage in the development of an industry. In our material it was generally only possible to judge this question qualitatively. Nevertheless I will offer a few examples.

In the wider field of nuclear energy, fuel cell plants and reactors, etc. generally represent subsystems in which only limited progress can now be expected. But there are still great advantages to be won, perhaps by further integration between power-supply systems in and between the various countries of Europe.

If we look at road transport we find that, taken separately, vehicles, road building and road maintenance represent fairly fully optimized subsystems. On the other hand there would probably be much to be gained from coordinating the construction and maintenance systems, from adapting the vehicle system more closely to the road system and, not least, from coordinating the transport system and the subsystems that generate the users of transport (location of industry, location of shopping centres, planning of working hours, etc.).

All those we spoke to in the Provincial Savings Bank agreed on the difficulty, if not impossibility, of discovering new services to offer the public—services that would make it possible to dominate a market. On the other hand much could have been done to coordinate the various subservices offered and to coordinate the internal 'production' subsystems.

The separate departments of the General Hospital functioned well as subsystems, but coordination between them and between the hospital and various external subsystems was extremely poor.

Postulate of Least Necessary Resources

Size of new system: Resources for exploitation of environment $> P$

To utilize a new system, whether it is geared to internal production or to some kind of product system, resources are required. The larger the system, the larger these resources will have to be. From this rule and the previous one it follows that greater resources will be accompanied by major advantages of scale. Thus, an organization which has to limit itself to small systems on account of its small resources, must possess greater inventiveness if it is to compete successfully with larger organizations.

The Construction and Building Company provides a simple but striking example. The company has succeeded in reducing production costs substantially. Although, technically, it is no more advanced than its competitors, it has integrated various components and subsystems in house building that have not previously been coordinated. One of its chief and amazingly simple devices has been to coordinate the work of preparing the ground with the actual work of house building. This success naturally roused a taste for more. Plans for a similar integration of town planning and house building have been mooted. At the same time the company has been working to develop systems to integrate customers' planning with the company's production set-up. This in turn has aroused interest in the problem of maintenance. Surely it would be attractive to the customer if the future maintenance of buildings could be shown to have been 'built into' their construction? All this time, however, the company has barely begun to exploit the advantages gained by the first steps in system development. Vast markets beyond the limited area where the company operates, seemed to be calling for exploitation. Should the next set of developments include the geographical dispersion of operations? 'Really, the company's too small for any more good ideas!' its president has declared.

Notes

1 These studies by members of SIAR have not yet been published.
2 Work on these projects continues.
3 Indented passages represent attempts to relate my arguments to the findings of other writers (generally organization theorists). These passages also provide illustrative examples, generally from our own case studies but sometimes from other sources as well.
4 Quoted from *Labor look at labor: A conversation*, published by the Center for the Study of Democratic Institutions, 1963.
5 The willingness of organizations to accept environmental values is strikingly illustrated by an experiment in small groups carried out by Zander, Medow and Elfron (1965).
6 I have intentionally used the terms organizational problems and the problems of organizations as synonyms. This conflicts with the common usage by which organizational problems mean internal difficulties in 'getting the organization to work'. According to my way of thinking, however, this is a misleading definition because an organization has to be judged on a basis of its ability to satisfy the demands of the environment. In referring to this more restricted class of problems I will use the term internal organizational problems.
7 The difference between reversible and irreversible changes is sometimes touched upon in the literature, e.g. in Sayles (1964) or Thompson (1967). However, the question of how this affects the problems of the business leader or the organization is usually left in the air, often because the issue is clouded by introducing the concept of short- and long-term changes.
8 The terms 'negative feedback' and 'positive feedback' are used here in their cybernetic sense. Some social psychologists misuse these expressions so that 'negative feedback' comes to mean something like a punishment and 'positive feedback' a reward.
9 See also Rhenman (1969).
10 Lawrence and Lorsch (1967) represents an excellent summary and includes much original empirical material.
11 These two possibilities do not form a dichotomy. A third possibility which I have not examined, is that the interaction between two subsystems leads to the creation of a new structure.
12 Lawrence and Lorsch (1967) refer to other writers who deal with similar ideas. Their own term is the 'fit' between two subsystems. The term 'consistency' has also been used in our earlier reports from SIAR.
13 It is only in the last few years that researchers have begun to show some interest in developing schemes for describing, and in some cases classifying, the environments of organizations. Emery and Trist (1965) have perhaps been the most ambitious. They classify environments according to dependencies between environmental components. They also discuss other features of the environment. I will look more closely at their suggestion in Appendix 4. For the present I will simply

mention some of the descriptive methods that we found helpful to an understanding of the organization.

[14] In the value environment I include rules (thou shalt and thou shalt not) and scales of values (yardsticks). von Wright (1963) has suggested a set of concepts which seems to suit this approach. A full description of an organization's value environment should include, at the least, an account of the content and the validity of the most important norms operating in the organization.

[15] We are not referring here to the Marxist theses of the disintegration of the state, but to later formulations of the convergence theory (cf. Smith and de Vyer, 1966). See in particular an essay by Oliver, H. M., Jr., *The concept and the classification of economic systems.*

[16] Johnsen (1968) emphasizes the conflicting nature of the values supported by an organization at any one time.

[17] The following figure shows the relations between the concepts used in Stymne's model. The numbers refer to seven postulates about the way the organization functions.

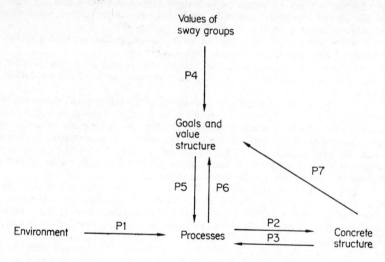

Illustration of postulates about how the organization functions

Sway groups in the organization can influence the values of other organization members. In this way they can affect the way in which the system functions. The one-way arrow at P4 indicates that the values of the sway groups must be treated in part as coming from outside the system. (Stymne, 1970, pp. 38–39)

[18] Some of these are illustrated in Stymne (1970) and Bruszt (1972a and b).

[19] See, e.g. March and Simon (1958), Rhenman, Strömberg and Westerlund (1970) and Lawrence and Lorsch (1967).

[20] An unpublished report by Sjöberg (1969) on an assignment for the National Swedish Pharmaceutical Laboratory has greatly contributed to my awareness of this problem.

[21] See Buckley (1967).

[22] This section is much influenced by Miller (1965a, b and c), although his subdivision differs from mine.

References

Ansoff, H. I. (1965). *Corporate Strategy*. McGraw-Hill, New York.
Argyris, C. (1962). *Interpersonal Competence and Organizational Effectiveness*. Irwin, Homewood, Ill.
Argyris, C. (1965). *Organization and Innovation*. Irwin, Homewood, Ill.
Argyris, C. [1967 (1953)]. *Executive Leadership: An Appraisal of a Manager in Action*. Harper and Row, New York.
Ashby, W. R. [1964 (1956)]. *An Introduction to Cybernetics*. Barnes and Noble Univ. Paperbacks, New York.
Bain, J. S. (1959). *Industrial Organization*. Wiley, New York.
Barnard, C. I. (1938). *The Functions of the Executive*. Harv. Univ. Press, Cambridge, Mass.
Baumol, W. J. (1959). *Business Behavior : Value and Growth*. Macmillan, New York.
Beaufre, A. (1966). *An Introduction to Strategy*. Faber, London.
Bell, D. (1967). The year 2000—The trajectory of an idea. *Daedalus*, **96**, 3, pp. 639–651.
Bennis, W. G. (1963). A new role for the behavioral sciences: Effecting organizational change. *Admin. Sci. Quart.*, **8**, 3, pp. 125–165.
Bennis, W. G. (1966). *Changing Organizations*. McGraw-Hill, New York.
Berg, C. (1969). *Erfarenheter av praktikfallsstudier av konflikter inom och mellan organisationer*. Stockholm (Mimeograph).
von Bertalanffy, L. (1955). General systems theory. *General Systems 1*, pp. 1–10.
Blake, R. R., *et al.* (1966). *Corporate Darwinism*. Gulf. Publ., Houston, Texas.
Blake, R. R., and Mouton, J. S. (1968). *Corporate Excellence through Grid Organizational Development*. Gulf Publ., Houston, Texas.
Borgenhammar, E. (1968). Läsa måste man—I och II. *Industria*, **68**, 2, pp. 60, 63, 90 and **68**, 3, pp. 58, 59, 90, 92–96.
Boulding, K. E. (1953). *The Organizational Revolution*. Harper and Row, New York.
Bright, J. R. (ed.), (1968). *Technological Forecasting for Industry and Government*. Prentice-Hall, Englewood Cliffs, N.J.
Bruszt, G. (1972a). *Några metodproblem vid studier av organisationers värderingsstruktur*. Stockholm: *SIAR-S-47*. (Mimeograph).
Bruszt, G. (1972b). *Situationsanpassade metoder för långsiktsplanering och organisationsutveckling i statsförvaltningen*. Stockholm: *SIAR-S-51*. (Not yet published) (Mimeograph).
Buckley, W. (1967). *Sociology and Modern Systems Theory*. Prentice-Hall, Englewood Cliffs, N.J.
Burnham, J. (1941). *The Managerial Revolution*. Longman, Toronto.
Burns, T. (1961). Research development and production—Problems of conflict and co-operation. *IRE Trans. on Eng. Mgmt*, **EM-8**, 1, pp. 15–23.

Burns, T., and Stalker, G. M. [1966 (1961)]. *The Management of Innovation*. Tavistock, London.

Chamberlain, N. W. (1968). *Enterprise and its Environment*. McGraw-Hill, New York.

Chandler, A. D., Jr. (1962). *Strategy and Structure*. The M.I.T. Press, Cambridge, Mass.

Commons, J. R. [1959 (1934)]. *Institutional Economics : Its Place in Political Economy*. Univ. of Wisc. Press, Madison, Wisc.

Cyert, R. M. and March, J. G. (1963). *A Behavioral Theory of the Firm*. Prentice-Hall, Englewood Cliffs, N.J.

Dalton, M. (1959). *Men who Manage*. Wiley, New York.

Dill, W. R. (1958). Environment as an influence on managerial autonomy. *Admin. Sci. Quart.* **2**, 4, pp. 409–443.

Drucker, P. (1955). *The Practice of Management*. Heinemann, London.

Elinder, E. (1966). Ar kyrkans kris ett marknadsföringsproblem? *Svenska Prästförbundets Årsprogram*, pp. 3–16.

Emery, F. E. (1967). The next thirty years: Concepts, methods and anticipations. *Hum. Rel.*, **20**, 3, p. 199 ff.

Emery, F. E., Thorsrud, E. and Lange, K. (1964). The Industrial Democracy Project. *Field Experiments at Christiania Spigerverk*. The Tavistock Inst. of Hum. Rel., London. (Work paper—Mimeograph).

Emery, F. E. and Trist, E. L. (1960). Socio-technical systems. *Proceedings, Management Science Models and Techniques*, vol. 2. 6th Annual International Meeting of the Institute of Management Sciences, London. (Also publ. in Emery, F. E. (ed.), *Systems Thinking*. Penguin, Harmondsworth, Middlesex, pp. 281–296.)

Emery, F. E. and Trist, E. L. (1965). The causal texture of organizational environments. *Hum. Rel.*, **18**, 1, pp. 21–23. (Also publ. in Emery, F. E. (ed.), *Systems Thinking*. Penguin, Harmondsworth, Middlesex, pp. 241–257.)

Fayol, H. [1949 (1916)]. *General and Industrial Management*. Pitman, London.

Ferguson, C. K. (1966). *Concerning the Nature of Human Systems and the Consultant's Role*. 24 October 1966. (Working paper—Mimeograph.)

Galbraith, J. K. (1967). *The New Industrial State*. Houghton, Boston.

Gouldner, A. W. (1954). *Patterns of Industrial Bureaucracy*. Free Press, Glencoe, Ill.

Granick, D. (1954). *Management of the Industrial Firm in the USSR*. Columbia Univ. Press, New York.

Granick, D. (1960). *The Red Executive*. Macmillan, London.

Guest, R. H. (1962). *Organizational Change; the Effect of Successful Leadership*. Irwin-Dorsey, Homewood, Ill.

Hellgren, C. H., *et al.* (1968). *Serviceföretaget—tre organisationsteoretiska synsätt*. Stockholm: *SIAR-S-15* (Mimeograph).

Hellgren, C. H. and Wirenhed, G. (1968). *Svensk sparbanksideologi 1947–1956*. Stockholm: *SIAR-S-14* (Mimeograph).

Henry, H. W. (1967). *Long Range Planning Practices in 45 Industrial Companies*. Prentice-Hall, Englewood Cliffs, N.J.

Hutte, H. (1968). *Sociatry of Work*. State Univ. of Groningen. (Draft—Mimeograph.)

Jantsch, E. (1967). *Technological Forecasting in Perspective*. OECD, Paris.

Jaques, E. (1951). *The Changing Culture of a Factory*. Tavistock, London.

Johnsen, E. (1968). *Studies in Multiobjective Decision Models.* Studentlitteratur, Lund. (Diss.)

Kahn, H. and Wiener, A. J. (1967). *The Year 2000. A Framework for Speculation on the Next Thirty-Three Years.* Macmillan, New York.

Kappel, F. R. (1960). *Vitality in a Business Enterprise.* McGraw-Hill, New York.

Katz, D. and Kahn, R. L. (1966). *The Social Psychology of Organizations.* Wiley, New York.

Katz, R. L. (1969). *Cases and Concepts in Corporate Strategy.* Prentice-Hall, Englewood Cliffs, N.J.

Kristensson, F. (1967). *Människor, företag och regioner.* Almqvist and Wiksell/ EFI, Stockholm.

Laing, R. D. (1961). *The Self and Others.* Tavistock, London.

Larsen, F. J. (1965). *Long-range Programming at Honeywell. European North American Conf. on Research Management.* Monte Carlo, 22–24 February, 1965. *DAS/RS/65.121.*

Lawrence, P. R. and Lorsch, J. W. (1967). *Organization and Environment. Managing Differentiation and Integration.* Harv. Univ., Boston.

Leavitt, H. J. (1965). Applied organizational change in industry: Structural, technological and humanistic approaches. March, J. G. (ed.), *Handbook of Organizations.* Rand McNally, Chicago, pp. 1144–1170.

Levitt, T. (1960). Marketing myopia. *Harv. Bus. Rev.*, **38**, 1, p. 45 ff.

Lorber, R. and Fladell, E. (1968). *The Gap.* McGraw-Hill, New York.

McGregor, D. (1960). *The Human Side of Enterprise.* McGraw-Hill, New York.

Mann, G. G. (1957). Studying and creating change: A means to understanding social organization. *Res. in Ind. Hum. Rel. 17.*

March, J. G. (ed.) (1965). *Handbook of Organizations.* Rand McNally, Chicago.

March, J. G. and Simon, H. A. (1958). *Organizations.* Wiley, New York.

Marcuse, H. (1964). *One-Dimensional Man.* Routledge and Kegan Paul, London.

Marrow, A. J., Bowers, D. G. and Seashore, S. E. (1967). *Management by Participation.* Harper and Row, New York.

Mayo, E. [1967 (1945)]. *Social Problems of an Industrial Civilization.* (rev. ed.) Harvard Univ., Grad. School of Bus. Admin., Boston.

Michels, R. [1962 (1911)]. *Political Parties: A Sociological Study of the Oligarchical Tendencies of Modern Democracy.* Collier, New York.

Miller, J. G. (1965a). Living systems: basic concepts. *Beh. Sci.*, **10**, 3, pp. 193–237.

Miller, J. G. (1965b). Living systems: structure and process. *Beh. Sci.*, **10**, 4, pp. 337–380.

Miller, J. G. (1965c). Living systems: cross-level hypotheses. *Beh. Sci.*, **10**, 4, pp. 380–411.

Morris, D. (1967). *The Naked Ape.* Cape, London.

Nilsson, G. (1971). *Företagsstrategier.* Gleerups, Lund. (*SIAR-S-40.*)

Normann, R. (1969). *Variation och omorientering. En studie av innovationsförmåga.* Stockholm: *SIAR-S-21* (Mimeograph).

Normann, R. (1972). *Organisationsstruktur och företags tillväxt.* Stockholm: *SIAR-S-46.* (Not yet published.) (Mimeograph.)

Oliver, H. M., Jr. (1966). The concept and the classification of economic systems. *Economic Systems and Public Policy.* Smith, R. S. and de Vyer, F. T. (ed.), Duke Univ. Press, Durham, N.C.

Olofsson, C. (1969). *Produktutveckling—Miljöförankring.* Stockholm: *SIAR-S-22.* (Mimeograph.)
Parsons, T. (1960). *Structure and Process in Modern Societies.* Free Press, Glencoe, Ill.
Pelz, D. C. and Andrews, F. M. (1966). *Scientists in Organizations.* Wiley, New York.
Penrose, E. T. (1959). *Theory of the Growth of the Firm.* Wiley, New York.
Perrow, C. (1968). Organizational goals. *Int. Encycl. of the Soc. Sci.,* Collier-Macmillan, New York, pp. 305–310.
Pfiffner, J. M. and Sherwood, F. P. (1960). *Administrative Organization.* Prentice-Hall, Englewood Cliffs, N.J.
Ramström, D. (1963). *Administrativa processer.* Bonniers, Stockholm.
Ramström, D. (1967). *The Efficiency of Control Strategies.* Almqvist and Wiksell, Stockholm. (Diss.)
Rhenman, E. (1964). *Företaget som ett styrt system.* EFI/Norstedts, Stockholm. (English version, 1966, *The Organization—a Controlled System.* Stockholm: *SIAR-1.* (Mimeograph).)
Rhenman, E. (1968a). *Industrial Democracy and Industrial Management.* Tavistock, London. (*SIAR-8.*) (Sw. ed. 1964.)
Rhenman, E. (1968b). *Organisationsplanering.* Scandinavian University Books, Stockholm. (*SIAR-S-13.*)
Rhenman, E. (1969). *Centrallasarettet—Systemanalys av ett svenskt sjukhus.* Studentlitteratur, Lund. (*SIAR-S-4.*)
Rhenman, E., Strömberg, L. and Westerlund, G. (1970). *Conflict and Co-operation in Business Organizations.* Wiley, London. (*SIAR-20.*) (First Sw. ed. 1963, Norstedts/EFI.)
Rhenman, E. and Stymne, B. (1965). *Företagsledning i en föränderlig värld.* Aldus, Stockholm.
Rhenman, E. and Wallis, R. (1967). '*Gamla sparbankens*' *särpräglade kompetens.* Stockholm: *AR-SIAR-45* (Mimeograph).
Rhenman, E., *et al.* (1967). *Personaladministrativa innovationer i skånska företag—En studie av organisationsstruktur och innovationstakt.* Stockholm: *SIAR-S-9.* (Mimeograph.)
Rothstein, J. (1958). *Communication, Organization and Science.* Keystone, Philadelphia.
Sandkull, B. (1968). *On Product Changes and Product Planning.* Studentlitteratur, Lund. (*SIAR-11.*)
Sandkull, B. and Stymne, B. (1968). *Ett fall för långsiktsplanering.* Stockholm: *AR-SIAR-62* (Mimeograph).
Sayles, L. R. (1964). *Managerial Behavior.* McGraw-Hill, New York.
Schon, D. A. (1967). *Technology and Change.* Delacorte Press, New York.
Selznick, P. (1949). *TVA and the Grass Roots.* Univ. of Calif. Press, Berkeley, Calif.
Selznick, P. (1957). *Leadership in Administration.* Row, Peterson, Evanston, Ill.
Shepard, H. A. (1965). Changing interpersonal and intergroup relationships in organizations. *Handbook of Organizations,* March, J. G. (ed.). Rand McNally, Chicago, pp. 1115–1143.
Sills, D. L. (1957). *The Volunteers—Means and Ends in a National Organization,* Free Press, Glencoe, Ill.
Simon, H. A. (1947). *Administrative Behavior.* Macmillan, New York.

Simon, H. A. (1953). Birth of an organization: The economic cooperation administration. *Pub. Admin. Rev.*, **13**, 4, pp. 227–236.

Sjöberg, L. (1969). (Stockholm, *SIAR*: Unpublished report.)

Smith, R. S. and de Vyer, F. T. (ed.) (1966). *Economic Systems and Public Policy*. Duke Univ. Press, Durham, N.C.

Starbuck, W. H. (1965). *Handbook of Organizations*. Rand McNally, Chicago, pp. 451–522.

Steiner, G. A. (1969). *Top Management Planning*. Macmillan, New York.

Stymne, B. (1966). EDP and organizational structure—A case study of an insurance company. *The Swed. J. of Econ.*, **68**, 2, pp. 89–116. (Also Stockholm, 1966, *SIAR-6* (Mimeograph).)

Stymne, B. (1967). *Mål, struktur och funktionssätt i tre organisationer*. Stockholm: *AR-SIAR-53* (Mimeograph).

Stymne, B. (1970). *Values and Processes. A Systems Study of Effectiveness in Three Organizations*. Studentlitteratur, Lund (*SIAR-17*) (Diss.).

Sutton, F. X., et al. (1956). *American Business Creed*. Harv. Univ. Press, Cambridge, Mass.

Taylor, F. W. [1947 (1911–12)]. *Scientific Management*. Harper, New York.

Thompson, J. D. (1967). *Organizations in Action*. McGraw-Hill, New York.

Tilles, S. (1966). *Making Strategy Explicit*. The Boston Consulting Group, Boston.

Tilles, S., *Strategic Planning in the Multi-Divisional Company*. The Boston Consulting Group, Boston. (Not dated.)

af Trolle, U. (1967). *Om tvånget att dö och konsten att överleva*. HHG/ Ekonomiskt Forum 30, Göteborg, pp. 3–8.

Wallroth, C. (1968a). An analysis of means–end structures. *Acta Sociol*, **11**, 1–2, pp. 110–118. (*SIAR-24*.)

Wallroth, C. (1968b). *Experiences in Organizational Change—Long-Range Planning in a Government Agency*. Stockholm: *SIAR-13* (Mimeograph).

Whyte, W. F. (1952). Economic incentives and human relations. *Harv. Bus. Rev.*, **30**, 2, p. 73 ff.

Whyte, W. F. and Hamilton, E. L. (1964). *Action Research for Management*. Irwin-Dorsey, Homewood, Ill.

Wodehouse, P. G. (1934). *Thank You, Jeeves*. Jenkins, London.

Votaw, D. (1964). *The Six-Legged Dog*. Univ. of Calif. Press, Berkeley.

von Wright, G. H. (1963). *Norm and Action*. Humanities Press, New York.

Zalesnik, A. (1966). *Human Dilemmas of Leadership*. Harper and Row, New York.

Zander, A., Medow, H. and Efron, R. (1965). Observers' expectations as determinants of group aspirations. *Hum. Rel.*, **18**, 3, pp. 273–287.

Zetterberg, H. L. (1962). *Social Theory and Social Practice*. The Bedminster Press, New York.

USA bygger : Insyn i amerikanska byggföretag, 1970. Byggförlaget, Stockholm. (*SIAR-S-34*.)

Index